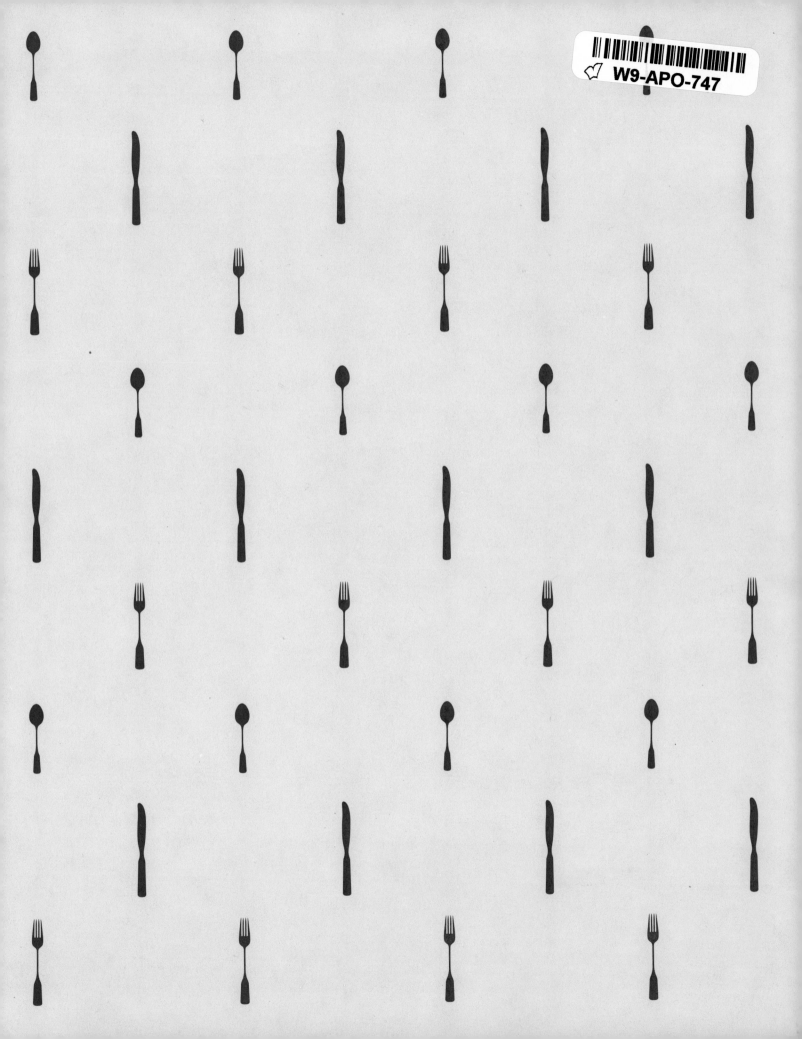

Fresh Ways
with Beef & Lamb

Time-Life Books Inc.
is a wholly owned subsidiary of
TIME INCORPORATED

FOUNDER: Henry R. Luce 1898-1967

Editor-in-Chief: Henry Anatole Grunwald
Chairman and Chief Executive Officer: J. Richard Munro
President and Chief Operating Officer: N. J. Nicholas Jr.
Chairman of the Executive Committee:
Ralph P. Davidson
Corporate Editor: Ray Cave
Executive Vice President, Books: Kelso F. Sutton
Vice President, Books: George Artandi

COVER
Toasted in a waffle iron, crisp pita bread encloses beef sirloin, red onions, tomatoes, mozzarella cheese and black olives. The recipe for this sandwich is found on page 70.

TIME-LIFE BOOKS INC.

EDITOR: George Constable
Director of Design: Louis Klein
Director of Editorial Resources: Phyllis K. Wise
Acting Text Director: Ellen Phillips
Editorial Board: Russell B. Adams Jr., Dale M. Brown, Roberta Conlan, Thomas H. Flaherty, Donia Ann Steele, Rosalind Stubenberg, Kit van Tulleken, Henry Woodhead
Director of Photography and Research:
John Conrad Weiser

PRESIDENT: Christopher T. Linen
Executive Vice President: John M. Fahey Jr.
Senior Vice Presidents: James L. Mercer, Leopoldo Toralballa
Vice Presidents: Stephen L. Bair, Ralph J. Cuomo, Terence J. Furlong, Neal Goff, Stephen L. Goldstein, Juanita T. James, Hallett Johnson III, Robert H. Smith, Paul R. Stewart
Director of Production Services: Robert J. Passantino

Editorial Operations
Copy Chief: Diane Ullius
Editorial Operations: Caroline A. Boubin (manager)
Production: Celia Beattie
Quality Control: James J. Cox (director)
Library: Louise D. Forstall

Correspondents: Elisabeth Kraemer-Singh (Bonn); Maria Vincenza Aloisi (Paris); Ann Natanson (Rome).

Column 1 (bottom):
6 on 7 Frutiger light w/6 pt. Frutiger Bold

Library of Congress Cataloguing in Publication Data
Main entry under title:
Fresh ways with beef and lamb.
    (Healthy home cooking)
    Includes index.
    1. Cookery (Beef) 2. Cookery (Lamb and mutton)
3. Microwave cookery. I. Time-Life Books. II. Title:
Fresh ways with beef and lamb. III. Series.
TX749.F756 1987   641.6'62   86-23118
ISBN 0-8094-5832-2
ISBN 0-8094-5833-0 (lib. bdg.)

For information on and a full description of any Time-Life Books series, please write:
Reader Information
Time-Life Books
541 North Fairbanks Court
Chicago, Illinois 60611

Time-Life Books Inc. offers a wide range of fine recordings, including a *Big Bands* series. For subscription information, call 1-800-621-7026, or write TIME-LIFE MUSIC, Time & Life Building, Chicago, Illinois 60611.

HEALTHY HOME COOKING

SERIES DIRECTOR: Dale M. Brown
Series Administrator: Elise Ritter Gibson
Designer (acting): Elissa E. Baldwin
Picture Editor: Sally Collins
Photographer: Renée Comet
Text Editor: Allan Fallow
Editorial Assistant: Rebecca C. Christoffersen

Editorial Staff for *Fresh Ways with Beef and Lamb:*
Book Manager: Susan Stuck
Associate Picture Editor: Scarlet Cheng
Researcher/Writers: Henry Grossi, Andrea Reynolds
Copy Coordinators: Elizabeth Graham, Ruth Baja Williams
Picture Coordinator: Linda Yates
Photographer's Assistant: Mazyar Parvaresh
Kitchen Assistant: Chhomaly Sok

Special Contributors: Mary Jane Blandford and Paula Sussman (food purchasing), Jeannette Smyth (text), Carol Gvozdich (nutrient analysis), Nancy Lendved (props), CiCi Williamson and Ann Steiner (microwave section), Rebecca Johns (recipes).

THE COOKS

LISA CHERKASKY has worked as a chef in Madison, Wisconsin, and in Washington, D.C., at Le Pavillon and Le Lion d'Or restaurants. She is a graduate of The Culinary Institute of America at Hyde Park, New York.

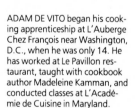

ADAM DE VITO began his cooking apprenticeship at L'Auberge Chez François near Washington, D.C., when he was only 14. He has worked at Le Pavillon restaurant, taught with cookbook author Madeleine Kamman, and conducted classes at L'Académie de Cuisine in Maryland.

JOHN T. SHAFFER is a graduate of The Culinary Institute of America. He has had broad experience as a chef, including five years at The Four Seasons Hotel in Washington, D.C., where he was *chef saucier* at Aux Beaux Champs restaurant.

THE CONSULTANT

CAROL CUTLER is the prizewinning author of many cookbooks; she also writes about food and entertaining for national magazines and newspapers. During the 12 years she lived in France, she studied at the Cordon Bleu and the École des Trois Gourmandes, as well as with private chefs. She is a member of the Cercle des Gourmettes, as well as a charter member and past president of Les Dames d'Escoffier.

THE NUTRITION CONSULTANT

JANET TENNEY has been involved in nutrition and consumer affairs since she received her master's degree in human nutrition from Columbia University. She is the manager for developing and implementing nutritional programs for a major chain of supermarkets in the Washington, D.C., area.

SPECIAL CONSULTANT

MARY JO FEENEY, who has a master's degree in nutrition from Case-Western Reserve University, is a registered dietician with 15 years of experience in the health-care field. She directs the education program of the California Beef Council. She is the author of the consumer information brochure *Light Cooking with Beef* and *California Beef*, a computerized cookbook.

Nutritional analyses for *Fresh Ways with Beef and Lamb* were derived from Practorcare's Nutriplanner System and other current data.

Other Publications:

FIX IT YOURSELF
FITNESS, HEALTH & NUTRITION
SUCCESSFUL PARENTING
UNDERSTANDING COMPUTERS
LIBRARY OF NATIONS
THE ENCHANTED WORLD
THE KODAK LIBRARY OF CREATIVE PHOTOGRAPHY
GREAT MEALS IN MINUTES
THE CIVIL WAR
PLANET EARTH
COLLECTOR'S LIBRARY OF THE CIVIL WAR
THE EPIC OF FLIGHT
THE GOOD COOK
WORLD WAR II
HOME REPAIR AND IMPROVEMENT
THE OLD WEST

This volume is one of a series of illustrated cookbooks that emphasize the preparation of healthful dishes for today's weight-conscious, nutrition-minded eaters.

Fresh Ways
with Beef & Lamb

BY

THE EDITORS OF TIME-LIFE BOOKS

TIME-LIFE BOOKS / ALEXANDRIA, VIRGINIA

Contents

Beef Curry

Japanese Simmered Beef

Garlic-Studded Lamb Shanks with Roasted Onions

2 Discovering Delicious Lamb 79

*Roast Leg of Lamb
with Pear Mustard*

Lime-Ginger Beef

3 Microwaving Beef and Lamb 121

The New, Lean Beef and Lamb

Mention red meat, and beef springs to mind, setting mouths to watering. Little wonder. Long America's favorite meat, beef remains so, with per capita consumption amounting to nearly 80 pounds a year. From a diner's point of view, beef offers real satisfaction — flavor, juiciness, wonderful texture with every chew. For the cook, beef can be as much fun to prepare as it is to eat, lending itself to a variety of cooking methods and happily uniting with a wide range of other foods. Still, beef consumption is down from what it once was: Health-minded Americans are eating less red meat and including more fish, chicken and complex carbohydrates in their diets.

This volume celebrates the old-fashioned virtues of beef and lamb, a red meat similar to beef in nutritional value and gaining rapidly in popularity. But the book does so in a modern way, concentrating on lean cuts cooked in little additional fat and served up in healthful three-ounce portions (each based on four ounces of trimmed raw meat). The recipes thus make it possible for lovers of beef and lamb to have their red meat and address their health concerns too.

In developing the 116 dishes that follow, the Time-Life cooks have heeded nutritionists' and the American Heart Association's recommendation that Americans cut down on the fat in their diet. Studies have shown that we obtain 40 percent of our calories from fat, and that we would be much better off if we reduced that amount to 30 percent or less. As the recipes will demonstrate, this is a goal that can be met by wisely selecting and preparing lean cuts of beef and lamb, without compromising taste or curtailing the pleasure both meats so abundantly offer. The cooks have been particularly careful to restrict the amount of saturated fat in their recipes, since it is this fat that raises levels of cholesterol in the blood and increases the risk of heart disease.

The nutritional aspects

Lean red meat is very good for you. Both beef and lamb are considered nutrient-dense foods, which means, simply, that they provide a high level of essential nutrients with relatively few calories. Three ounces of cooked lean beef — which has just 181 calories — supplies 46 percent of the protein, 76 percent of the vitamin B_{12}, 20 percent of the niacin and 40 percent of the zinc an adult male should have in his daily diet. That same portion also provides 27 percent of his daily iron requirement. And because 40 to 60 percent of the iron is heme iron, which is readily absorbed by the body, beef has particular importance to women, for whom iron ranks high among the essential minerals. Moreover, heme iron enhances the body's ability to absorb iron from other foods.

Contrary to what most people believe, red meat is not overloaded with cholesterol. A three-ounce serving of beef, for example, averages 73 milligrams of cholesterol, a quarter of the amount a healthy individual may have in the course of a day's eating. Most meats and some fish have cholesterol levels comparable to beef.

For our dishes, we have chosen beef and lamb cuts (diagrams, page 9) from the least fatty parts of the animals, namely the more muscular tissue. Yet it is fat, of course, that gives meat much of its flavor and juiciness. Because we have avoided the fattier cuts, we have employed methods and ingredients that ensure flavor and moistness. And we have been very careful not to overcook the meat, which is easy to do with lean cuts, particularly when pieces are small. Prolonged high heat is the surest way to toughen meat — and to dry it out and shrink it as well.

For roasting, broiling and grilling, we recommend that the meat be cooked medium rare. This can be ascertained by inserting a meat thermometer into the thickest part of the meat and letting the temperature reach 140° F. (Such a temperature also guarantees that harmful organisms that might be present will be killed.) An instant-reading thermometer, which registers temperatures just 10 seconds after insertion, can be very handy, especially when the piece is small. After the desired 140° F. temperature has been reached, let the meat rest away from the heat for about 15 minutes, during which time its internal temperature will rise five more degrees — just right for medium-rare meat.

Because the recipes call for scant cooking oil, we urge the use of nonstick skillets wherever possible. To further keep down calories and to restrict saturated fat, we make little use of cream, butter and cheese in sauces. Any fat that may have melted out of the meat is discarded. We obtain smooth, flavorful sauces by cooking down the liquids in which the meat and other ingredients simmered, thus retaining their nutrients.

With tougher cuts, we may pound the meat to tenderize it. By carving diagonally across the grain, we produce slices that are easy to chew. Sometimes we cut meat into small pieces or strips so that they can cook quickly. For stir frying, the raw meat is sliced into thin strips and tossed in a wok or skillet, then removed and replaced by the vegetables called for in the dish. Only when the vegetables are ready is the meat returned to the vessel and reheated, a measure that keeps it from overcooking and turning leathery. We do not salt the meat before grilling, roasting or broiling it because salt draws out the juices, producing dry meat.

Reshaping the animals themselves

Thanks to the meat industry's efforts, beef and lamb are leaner than they used to be. About half the beef cattle now raised spend more time eating grass and less time being finished, or fattened, on grain. Ranchers are seeking to establish leaner breeds through crossbreeding. Even the Longhorn, with which the American beef industry can be said to have started, is undergoing scrutiny as a possible progenitor of a new slim breed. "We're looking for an animal that is shaped like a barrel, without much fat on it," says one cattle buyer. "That means it will be meaty."

Until meat from such transformed animals begins reaching the market in quantity, look for the lean cuts now available. Many butchers remove excess fat, sometimes trimming to within an eighth of an inch of the flesh. Buy trimmed meat and further trim it at home. Bear in mind that the market grade "prime" signifies fattier meat — it is prime because of the amount of fat marbling the tissue. Most of this grade goes to the restaurant trade. We have concentrated on the leaner "choice," and on "good," which is usually sold under a store- or house-brand name as economy meat. "Good" is as nutritious as the other grades and is often recommended to people on fat-restricted diets.

For lamb to be labeled lamb, it must come from an animal that is less than a year old; most lamb sold here is six to eight months old. Thanks to improvements in breeding and raising them, American lambs are twice as big as lambs produced elsewhere.

Storing beef and lamb

Both meats are less perishable than poultry and fish. They can be kept for up to four days in the plastic wrappers in which they were bought. However, ground meat should never be kept longer than two to three days. Many people who intend to store meat in the refrigerator for more than a couple of days prefer to repackage it. Roasts, steaks and chops should be rewrapped loosely in wax paper, not plastic, then set on a plate or platter to catch any juices. When wrapped tightly in clinging plastic, the meat's surface remains moist, encouraging bacterial growth. Loose wrapping allows air to circulate, thus eliminating the damp environment bacteria must have to thrive. Meat so wrapped can be stored for up to four days providing the refrigerator's temperature is colder than 40° F. In purchasing meat, be sure to look at the so-called pull date on the label, the date beyond which the meat may not be sold. Bought on the pull date itself, the meat may still be stored in the refrigerator.

Preparing meat for freezing involves wrapping it tightly in water- or vapor-proof plastic, aluminum foil or freezer paper, then squeezing all air from the package. Air pockets cause freezer burn, which dries out meat and alters its color and texture. Properly wrapped beef may be kept in a freezer for up to a year and lamb for nine months, providing they are quickly frozen and maintained at 0° F. or lower. Ground meat should not be kept longer than three months.

About the book's organization

This book falls into three sections, with the first and second devoted to beef and lamb respectively, and the last to preparing both with the aid of a microwave oven. The recipes in each of the first two sections are grouped according to the primary cooking method called for, and most come with suggestions for accompanying vegetables or starches.

Such dry-heat methods as grilling and roasting are generally applied to tender roasts and chops. Braising and other moist-heat methods are reserved mostly for tougher cuts. Vegetables are often cooked with the meat to provide moisture as well as flavor; and herbs and spices, fruits and fruit juices, wines and spirits are called upon to increase the savor of the dishes, all of which are low in salt. Many of the recipes ask for unsalted brown stock or unsalted chicken stock (recipes, page 137). Canned stock may be substituted for the homemade variety, but if it is salted, be sure to omit the salt from the recipe. A glossary toward the end of the volume identifies and describes any ingredients or techniques that may be unfamiliar.

Our dishes not only take into account your concerns about fat but also provide information about nutrition in general. Printed beside each recipe is a breakdown of the nutrients it contains. This analysis should make it easier for you to plan the rest of your meal — and the other menus for the day as well — so that you can meet the healthful goal of having fewer of the calories you consume come from fat.

The Key to Better Eating

Healthy Home Cooking addresses the concerns of today's weight-conscious, health-minded cooks with recipes developed within strict nutritional guidelines.

The chart at right presents the National Research Council's Recommended Dietary Allowances of both calories and protein for healthy men, women and children of average size, along with the council's recommendations for the "safe and adequate" maximum intake of sodium. Although the council has not established similar recommendations for either cholesterol or fat, the chart does include what the National Institutes of Health and the American Heart Association consider the maximum allowable amounts of these in one day's eating by healthy members of the general population.

The volumes in the Healthy Home Cooking series do not purport to be diet books, nor do they focus on health foods. Rather, the books express a commonsense approach to cooking that uses salt, sugar, cream, butter and oil in moderation while including other ingredients that contribute flavor and satisfaction as well. The portions themselves are modest in size.

The recipes make few unusual demands. Naturally they call for fresh ingredients, offering substitutes should these be unavailable. (Only the original ingredient is calculat-

Recommended Dietary Guidelines

		Average Daily Intake		Maximum Daily Intake			
		CALORIES	PROTEIN grams	CHOLESTEROL milligrams	TOTAL FAT grams	SATURATED FAT grams	SODIUM milligrams
Children	7-10	2400	22	240	80	27	1800
Females	11-14	2200	37	220	73	24	2700
	15-18	2100	44	210	70	23	2700
	19-22	2100	44	300	70	23	3300
	23-50	2000	44	300	67	22	3300
	51-75	1800	44	300	60	20	3300
Males	11-14	2700	36	270	90	30	2700
	15-18	2800	56	280	93	31	2700
	19-22	2900	56	300	97	32	3300
	23-50	2700	56	300	90	30	3300
	51-75	2400	56	300	80	27	3300

ed in the nutrient analysis, however.) Most of the ingredients can be found in any well-stocked supermarket; the occasional exceptions can be bought in specialty shops or ethnic food stores.

About cooking times

To help the cook plan ahead effectively, Healthy Home Cooking takes time into account in all its recipes. While recognizing that everyone cooks at a different speed, and that stoves and ovens may differ somewhat in their temperatures, the series provides ap-

proximate "working" and "total" times for every dish. Working time stands for the minutes actively spent on preparation; total time includes unattended cooking time, as well as time devoted to marinating, steeping or soaking various ingredients. Because the recipes emphasize fresh foods, the dishes may take a bit longer to prepare than those in "quick and easy" cookbooks that call for canned or packaged products, but the payoff in flavor, and often in added nutritional value, should compensate for the little extra time involved.

Guaranteeing Lean Ground Every Time

All ground meat is not created equal. And what is labeled "lean" in the supermarket may not be as low in fat as you would like. There is a way, however, to guarantee a very lean product — buy a lean cut, and ask the butcher to trim and grind it for you.

Throughout this book, the recipes based on ground beef call for beef round. Top, bottom or eye round trimmed of fat and then ground has only 37 percent of its calories in fat — well within the 45 percent that nutritionists recommend. Supermarket ground lamb is usually made from the fattier cuts, and is best avoided. But lamb ground from leg or loin guarantees a lean product.

Once you have selected a lean cut, ask the butcher to trim and

grind it, or, if you like, you can prepare it at home, either chopping it by hand, grinding it with a meat grinder or chopping it in a food processor.

To hand-chop beef or lamb, divide the meat along the muscle seams into sections, paring away all sinewy tissue. Trim off fat and membrane, and cut the meat into small cubes of roughly equal size. Spread the meat out evenly on a cutting board and, with a cleaver or a heavy chef's knife, chop the meat, using a rhythmical motion. As you chop, the meat will spread out. To achieve a consistent texture, stop from time to time and scrape the outer edges of meat back into the center, turning the mass over each time you do so.

The Leanest of the Lean

These diagrams show and identify the beef and lamb cuts *(colored areas)* that are used in this book. No cut derives more than 45 percent of its calories from fat, and many come in well under that amount.

Lamb

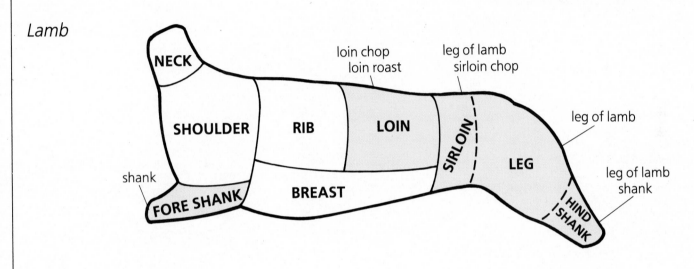

Beef

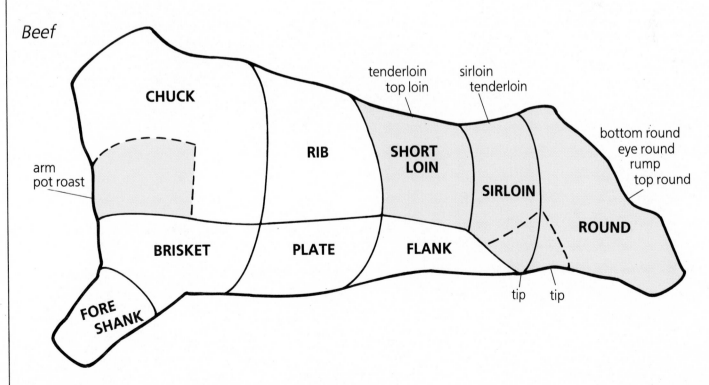

1 Beef that has been trimmed of fat and freshly ground is ready to play a starring role in a lightened version of an Italian-style pasta dish (recipe, page 73).

Beef's Eternal Appeal

Beef is robust meat. It can be served on its own, with very little fuss. A broiled or charcoal-grilled steak has singular appeal. But beef is also a meat that lends itself to a variety of preparations. This is particularly true of the leaner cuts called for by the 63 recipes in this section. While the dishes depend on beef's rich flavor, they often include other ingredients, especially vegetables. A delicious mutual blending then occurs, the beef's juices marrying the juices of the mushrooms, root vegetables or greens, to the enhancement of all. Similarly, a judicious sprinkling of herbs or other flavorings such as citrus zests can elevate the character of a beef dish.

The measure of a good piece of beef has long been marbling, the fine distribution of fat throughout the meat. But in these more health-conscious times, shoppers are increasingly turning away from such meat. That is why this book ignores rib roasts, short ribs, blade roasts and skirt steaks, among others; their fat content is simply too high for the conscientious cook eager to have no more than 30 percent of the calories for the day coming from fat. Even flank steak, which long had a reputation for being lean, has been shown by the Department of Agriculture to contain more than 15 percent fat by weight, which means that 55 percent of its calories come from fat, 10 percentage points more than the 45 percent maximum for this book.

That still leaves plenty of cuts to choose from. When buying lean beef today, look for pieces that are firm to the touch, with a fine texture or grain and a bright red color. Vacuum-packed beef will appear darker because it has been protected from air, but will redden once the plastic wrapper is removed. And remember, it is not only the quality of the meat that counts, but the quality of the cooking. Be careful not to overcook lean beef; the recipes that follow are precise in their cooking times.

Grilled Sirloin Steak with Peach Piccalilli

Serves 6
Working time: about 20 minutes
Total time: about 45 minutes

Calories **205**
Protein **24g.**
Cholesterol **66mg.**
Total fat **7g.**
Saturated fat **3g.**
Sodium **185mg.**

one 1¾-lb. boneless sirloin steak, about 1 inch thick, trimmed of fat
2 tsp. chopped fresh ginger
⅛ tsp. cayenne pepper
¼ tsp. salt
Peach piccalilli
1 white onion (about ½ lb.)
2 large ripe peaches (about ¾ lb.)
½ tbsp. safflower oil
1 tsp. chopped fresh ginger
⅛ tsp. cayenne pepper
3 tbsp. red wine vinegar
⅛ tsp. salt
¼ cup fresh orange juice
1½ tbsp. chopped fresh cilantro or parsley

To start the piccalilli, slice the onion in half lengthwise . Cutting with the grain, slice each onion half into strips about ¼ inch wide. Blanch the peaches in boiling wa-

ter for 30 seconds, then remove them with a slotted spoon. When the peaches are cool enough to handle, peel and pit them; cut the peaches into thin slices.

Heat the oil in a large, nonstick skillet over medium-low heat. Add the onion, ginger and cayenne pepper and cook the onion until it is translucent — seven to 10 minutes. Stir in the vinegar and salt, then cook the mixture for one minute more. Add the peaches and orange juice. Cook the piccalilli slowly, until the peaches are soft but not mushy — an additional 12 to 15 minutes. Remove the skillet from the heat and stir in the cilantro or parsley.

If you plan to grill the steak, start the coals about 30 minutes before cooking time; to broil, preheat the broiler for 10 minutes. With your fingers, rub the ginger and cayenne pepper into both sides of the steak, and allow it to stand at room temperature until you are ready to cook it.

Cook the steak on the first side for six minutes, then turn it, and sprinkle it with the salt. Grill the steak on the second side for five or six minutes for medium-rare meat. Transfer the steak to a platter and let it rest for about five minutes before carving it into thin slices. Serve the peach piccalilli on the side.

SUGGESTED ACCOMPANIMENTS: *sugar snap peas; wild rice.*

Beef Salad
with Carrots and Mint

Serves 6
Working time: about 40 minutes
Total time: about 3 hours (includes marinating)

Calories **255**
Protein **25g.**
Cholesterol **63mg.**
Total fat **11g.**
Saturated fat **3g.**
Sodium **340mg.**

one 1¾-lb. top round steak, trimmed of fat
¼ cup unsalted brown stock or unsalted chicken stock (recipes, page 137)
1½ tbsp. low-sodium soy sauce
¼ cup fresh lime juice
2 garlic cloves, finely chopped
2 tsp. sugar
freshly ground black pepper
2 tsp. chili paste, or ½ tsp. hot red-pepper flakes
2 tbsp. chopped fresh mint, or 2 tsp. dried mint
3 carrots
1 cucumber, preferably unwaxed, thinly sliced
1 sweet white onion, thinly sliced
6 cherry tomatoes, halved
2 cups shredded daikon radish or regular radish
2 tbsp. safflower oil

Set the steak in a baking dish. In a small bowl, combine the stock, soy sauce, 2 tablespoons of the lime juice, the garlic, sugar, some black pepper, the chili paste or pepper flakes, and half of the mint. Pour this mixture over the steak and let it marinate at room temperature for two hours.

With a channel knife or a paring knife, cut several shallow lengthwise grooves in each carrot. Thinly slice the carrots and place the resulting flowers in a large bowl. Add the cucumber, onion, tomatoes and radish to the bowl with the carrots.

Remove the steak from the marinade and pat it dry with paper towels. Strain the marinade into a small saucepan and bring it to a boil. Remove the pan from the heat, whisk in the oil and the remaining 2 tablespoons of lime juice, and pour the dressing over the vegetables. Add the rest of the mint and toss well. Set the vegetables aside.

Broil the steak about 3 inches below a preheated broiler until it is medium rare — five to seven minutes per side. Transfer the steak to a cutting board and let it rest for 10 minutes, then slice it against the grain into thin pieces.

Using a slotted spoon, transfer the vegetables to a serving dish. Arrange the steak slices on top of the vegetables; pour the dressing left in the bowl over all, and serve at once.

SUGGESTED ACCOMPANIMENT: *poppy-seed rolls.*

Grilled Top Loin Steaks with Glazed Shallots and Mushrooms

Serves 4
Working time: about 20 minutes
Total time: about 40 minutes

Calories **290**	2 top loin steaks (about 10 oz. each), trimmed of fat and cut into 2 pieces
Protein **26g.**	
Cholesterol **61mg.**	2 tsp. safflower oil
Total fat **9g.**	½ lb. mushrooms, wiped clean
Saturated fat **3g.**	½ lb. shallots, peeled
Sodium **210mg.**	2 tbsp. honey
	1 tsp. chopped fresh tarragon, or ½ tsp. dried tarragon
	½ cup Madeira or port
	½ cup unsalted brown stock or unsalted chicken stock (recipes, page 137)
	2 tsp. cornstarch mixed with 1 tbsp. of the stock
	¼ tsp. salt
	freshly ground black pepper

If you plan to grill the steaks, prepare the coals about 30 minutes before cooking time; to broil, preheat the broiler for 10 minutes.

Heat the oil in a nonstick skillet over medium heat; add the mushrooms and sauté them until they are lightly browned — about four minutes. Using a slotted spoon, transfer the mushrooms to a bowl. Pour 1 cup of water into the skillet and add the shallots, honey and tarragon. Partially cover the skillet; bring the liquid to a simmer and cook the mixture until the shallots are translucent and only ¼ cup of liquid remains — eight to 10 minutes.

Return the mushrooms to the skillet and toss them with the shallots and the liquid until all are coated with a syrupy glaze — about two minutes longer. Keep the glazed shallots and mushrooms warm.

In a small saucepan, reduce the Madeira or port by half over medium-high heat. Add the stock and bring the mixture to a simmer. Whisk the cornstarch mixture into the simmering liquid. Continue cooking the sauce until it thickens, and add ⅛ teaspoon of the salt and some pepper. Keep the sauce warm while you prepare the steaks.

Grill or broil the steaks for three minutes. Turn the steaks over and season them with the remaining ⅛ teaspoon of salt and some more pepper. Cook the steaks for three minutes longer for medium-rare meat. Serve the steaks with the glazed shallots and mushrooms on the side and the sauce poured on top.

SUGGESTED ACCOMPANIMENT: *steamed green beans.*

Low-Fat Hamburgers with Spicy Pumpkin Ketchup

THE RECIPE FOR PUMPKIN KETCHUP YIELDS MORE THAN
ENOUGH FOR EIGHT HAMBURGERS; THE EXCESS MAY BE STORED
IN THE REFRIGERATOR FOR UP TO ONE WEEK.

Serves 8
Working time: about 15 minutes
Total time: about 1 hour and 15 minutes

Calories **275**	1¾ lb. beef round, trimmed of fat and ground (box, page 8)
Protein **21g.**	
Cholesterol **47mg.**	1⅓ cups bulgur
Total fat **5g.**	2 garlic cloves, very finely chopped
Saturated fat **2g.**	⅓ cup finely chopped fresh parsley
Sodium **155mg.**	2 tbsp. grainy mustard
	Spicy pumpkin ketchup
	16 oz. canned pumpkin (1½ cups)
	1 onion, finely chopped
	1 apple or pear, peeled, cored and chopped
	½ cup cider vinegar
	2 tbsp. sugar
	1 tbsp. honey
	½ tsp. ground cloves
	½ tsp. curry powder
	¼ tsp. ground allspice
	¼ tsp. cayenne pepper
	¼ tsp. salt
	freshly ground black pepper

Combine the ketchup ingredients in a nonreactive saucepan. Stir in 1 cup of water and simmer the mixture over medium-low heat for one hour. Purée the ketchup in a food processor or a blender, then work it through a sieve with a wooden spoon. Transfer the ketchup to a serving bowl and set it aside.

While the ketchup is simmering, put the bulgur into a heatproof bowl and pour 1⅔ cups of boiling water ▶

over it. Cover the bowl and set it aside for 30 minutes.

If you plan to grill the hamburgers, prepare the coals about 30 minutes before cooking time; to broil, pre-heat the broiler for 10 minutes.

Put the ground beef, soaked bulgur, garlic, parsley and mustard into a bowl, and combine them thoroughly by hand. Form the mixture into eight patties. Grill or broil the hamburgers for three to four minutes on each side for medium-rare meat. Serve the hamburgers hot with the ketchup alongside.

SUGGESTED ACCOMPANIMENTS: *poppy-seed rolls; sliced tomatoes; lettuce leaves.*

Sirloin Grilled in Garlic Smoke

Serves 6
Working time: about 30 minutes
Total time: about 45 minutes

Calories **220**
Protein **26g.**
Cholesterol **76mg.**
Total fat **11g.**
Saturated fat **3g.**
Sodium **105mg.**

one 2-lb. boneless sirloin steak, about 1½ inches thick, trimmed of fat
10 unpeeled garlic cloves, crushed
Onion-pepper relish
2 tbsp. safflower oil
1 small red onion, thinly sliced
1 garlic clove, finely chopped
1 tsp. finely chopped fresh ginger
1 green pepper, seeded, deribbed and julienned
2 scallions, trimmed and thinly sliced
2 tbsp. rice vinegar or distilled white vinegar
¼ tsp. sugar
⅛ tsp. salt

About 30 minutes before cooking time, prepare the coals in an outdoor grill. Put the crushed garlic cloves in 1 cup of cold water and let them soak while you make the relish.

Heat the oil in a heavy-bottomed or nonstick skillet over medium heat. Add the red-onion slices and cook them, stirring frequently, until they have softened without losing their color — three to four minutes. Add the chopped garlic and ginger, and cook the mixture for 30 seconds longer; transfer it to a bowl. Add the green pepper, scallions, vinegar, sugar and salt; stir the relish and set it aside.

When the coals are hot, grill the steak for seven minutes on the first side. Drain the water from the garlic cloves. Remove the steak from the grill and toss the soaked garlic cloves directly onto the coals; a garlicky smoke will curl up. Return the steak to the grill and cook it on the second side for five to seven minutes longer for medium-rare meat.

Transfer the steak to a platter and let it rest for five minutes. Carve the steak into thin slices; spread the onion-pepper relish over each portion just before serving, or present the relish on the side.

SUGGESTED ACCOMPANIMENT: *baked potatoes.*

Grilled Top Loin Steaks with Fennel-Scented Vegetables

Serves 8
Working time: about 20 minutes
Total time: about 40 minutes

Calories **235**
Protein **26g.**
Cholesterol **65mg.**
Total fat **10g.**
Saturated fat **39g.**
Sodium **200mg.**

4 top loin steaks (about 10 oz. each), trimmed of fat
2 tbsp. olive oil
1½ tsp. fennel seeds, lightly crushed
3 garlic cloves, very thinly sliced
1 lb. eggplant, cut into ½-inch cubes
1 cup chopped onion
2 tbsp. fresh lemon juice
1½ lb. ripe tomatoes, peeled, seeded and cut into ½-inch pieces
½ tsp. salt
freshly ground black pepper

If you plan to grill the steaks, prepare the coals in an outdoor grill about 30 minutes before cooking time; to broil, preheat the broiler for about 10 minutes.

In the meantime, heat the olive oil in a large, heavy-bottomed skillet over high heat. When the oil is hot, add the fennel seeds and garlic, and cook them for 30 seconds, stirring constantly. Add the eggplant, onion and lemon juice and cook the vegetables for five minutes, stirring frequently. Next, add the tomatoes, ¼ teaspoon of the salt and a generous grinding of pepper to the skillet. Cook the vegetable mixture for three or four minutes longer, stirring continuously. Cover the skillet and set the mixture aside while you finish the dish.

Grill or broil the steaks for three to four minutes. Turn the steaks over and sprinkle them with the remaining ¼ teaspoon salt and some pepper. Cook the steaks for an additional three to four minutes for medium-rare meat. Let the steaks stand for five minutes before thinly slicing them against the grain. Divide the meat and vegetables among eight dinner plates and serve at once.

SUGGESTED ACCOMPANIMENT: *steamed red potatoes.*

Grilled Roulades
with Onion Compote

Serves 4
Working time: about 45 minutes
Total time: about 1 hour

Calories **230**
Protein **21g.**
Cholesterol **44mg.**
Total fat **5g.**
Saturated fat **2g.**
Sodium **305mg.**

4 eye round steaks (about 1 lb.), trimmed of fat
1¼ lb. pearl onions, blanched in boiling water for five minutes, drained and peeled
½ cup golden raisins
⅛ tsp. salt
1 tsp. red wine vinegar
¼ cup grainy mustard
¼ cup finely chopped fresh parsley
freshly ground black pepper

Put the onions, raisins, salt, vinegar and 1 cup of water into a heavy-bottomed saucepan. Bring the liquid to a

boil, then reduce the heat, and simmer the mixture until the onions are golden brown and the liquid has evaporated — 15 to 20 minutes.

If you plan to grill the roulades, prepare the coals about 30 minutes before cooking time; to broil, pre-heat the broiler for about 10 minutes.

While the onion compote is reducing, butterfly and pound the steaks as shown on page 19. Mix the mustard, parsley and some pepper in a small bowl and spread this mixture over the meat. Roll each steak into a loose bundle; tie the roulades with butcher's twine to hold them together.

When the onions finish cooking, set them aside and keep them warm.

Grill or broil the beef rolls for a total of eight minutes, turning them every two minutes. Transfer the rolls to a platter; serve the onion compote alongside.

SUGGESTED ACCOMPANIMENT: *steamed Brussels sprouts.*

Butterflying and Pounding a Steak

1 *BUTTERFLYING A STEAK. Place a steak flat on the work surface and steady it by pressing it down with one hand. With your other hand, use a thin-bladed knife (here, a slicer) to halve the steak horizontally, stopping just short of the edge so that the two halves remain attached, like the wings of a butterfly.*

2 *POUNDING THE MEAT. Unfold the steak and place it on a square of plastic wrap. Cover it with another piece of wrap. Using the smooth end of a meat mallet or the flat of a large, heavy knife, pound the meat to the thickness called for by the recipe.*

Grilled Beef Tenderloin Steaks with Roasted Garlic Sauce

Serves 4
Working time: about 30 minutes
Total time: about 50 minutes

Calories **170**
Protein **20g.**
Cholesterol **55mg.**
Total fat **6g.**
Saturated fat **2g.**
Sodium **100mg.**

four 4-oz. beef tenderloin steaks
2 whole garlic bulbs, cloves separated but not peeled
½ tsp. juniper berries, crushed
1 tsp. cracked peppercorns
1 cup red wine
3 shallots, sliced, or ½ small onion, finely chopped
2 cups unsalted brown stock or unsalted chicken stock (recipes, page 137)

Preheat the oven to 500° F.

Scatter the garlic cloves in a small baking dish and roast them until they are very soft — 20 to 30 minutes. Set the garlic cloves aside to cool.

If you plan to grill the steaks, prepare the coals about 30 minutes before cooking time; to broil, preheat the broiler for about 10 minutes.

In a small bowl, mix together the juniper berries and pepper. Press the mixture into both sides of each of the steaks and set them aside at room temperature.

Pour the wine into a small, nonreactive saucepan and add the shallots or onion. Boil the mixture over medium-high heat until nearly all the liquid has evaporated — about five minutes. Add the stock, bring the liquid to a boil, and continue cooking it until it is reduced to about 1 cup — approximately five minutes.

Squeeze the garlic pulp from the skins into a food processor or a blender. Pour in the stock and purée the garlic. Put the garlic sauce (it will be thick) into the saucepan and keep it warm.

Cook the steaks for approximately three minutes on each side for medium-rare meat. Serve the steaks with the garlic sauce.

SUGGESTED ACCOMPANIMENT: *oven-fried potatoes.*

South Seas Kebabs

Serves 4
Working time: about 35 minutes
Total time: about 2 hours and 30 minutes
(includes marinating)

Calories **180**
Protein **19g.**
Cholesterol **44mg.**
Total fat **4g.**
Saturated fat **2g.**
Sodium **195mg.**

1 lb. eye round, trimmed of fat and cut into ¾-inch cubes
1 ripe papaya, peeled, seeded and cut into 1-inch cubes
1 sweet red or green pepper, seeded, deribbed
and cut into ¾-inch squares
Honey-ginger glaze
¾ cup unsalted brown stock or unsalted chicken stock (recipes, page 137)
1 scallion, trimmed and thinly sliced
2 garlic cloves, finely chopped
2 tbsp. finely chopped fresh ginger
1 tbsp. honey
¼ tsp. salt
¼ tsp. cracked black peppercorns
1 tbsp. cornstarch, mixed with 1 tbsp. water

Purée about one third of the papaya in a food processor or a blender; set the remaining cubes aside. Mix the beef and the papaya purée in a shallow dish; cover the dish and marinate the beef in the refrigerator for about two hours.

If you plan to grill the kebabs, prepare the coals about 30 minutes before cooking time. To broil, preheat the broiler for 10 minutes.

To prepare the glaze, combine the stock, scallion, garlic, ginger, honey, salt and cracked peppercorns in a small saucepan over medium heat. Bring the mixture to a simmer and cook it for three to four minutes. Stir in the cornstarch mixture and continue cooking and stirring the glaze until it thickens — one to two minutes. Remove the glaze from the heat and set it aside.

To assemble the kebabs, thread the cubes of beef, papaya and pepper onto four 12-inch skewers. Cook the kebabs for three minutes. Turn them and cook them for three minutes more. Brush some glaze over the kebabs and cook them for one minute. Turn the kebabs once more, brush them with the glaze, and cook them for another minute. Transfer the kebabs to a serving platter and brush them with the remaining glaze; serve the kebabs immediately.

SUGGESTED ACCOMPANIMENT: *saffron rice tossed with peas.*

Marinated Beef Salad with Potatoes and Green Beans

Serves 4
Working time: about 25 minutes
Total time: about 3 hours (includes marinating)

Calories **295**
Protein **29g.**
Cholesterol **76mg.**
Total fat **11g.**
Saturated fat **3g.**
Sodium **150mg.**

one 1¼-lb. boneless sirloin steak, about 1-inch thick, trimmed of fat
1 small onion, thinly sliced
1 garlic clove, finely chopped
½ green pepper, finely chopped
⅛ tsp. cracked black peppercorns
1 tbsp. fresh tarragon, chopped, or 1 tsp. dried tarragon
juice of 2 lemons
½ lb. boiling potatoes, scrubbed and cut into 1-inch cubes
¾ lb. green beans, trimmed
⅛ tsp. salt
1 ripe tomato, cut into wedges
4 tsp. safflower oil
1 tsp. Dijon mustard

In a small bowl, combine the onion, garlic, green pepper, black peppercorns and tarragon. Scatter half of the mixture on the bottom of a shallow nonreactive pan. Put the steak into the pan and sprinkle the rest of the mixture on top. Pour the lemon juice over the steak and let it marinate for two hours at room temperature or overnight in the refrigerator.

Cook the potatoes in a saucepan of boiling water until they are tender — seven to 10 minutes. Drain them and set them aside to cool. Pour enough water into the saucepan to fill it to a depth of 1 inch. Set a steamer in the pan and bring the water to a boil over medium-high heat. Add the beans to the steamer, cover the pan, and steam the beans until they are just tender — about 5 minutes. Refresh the beans under cold running water, drain them well, and put them into a large salad bowl.

Preheat the broiler. Remove the steak from the marinade and pour the marinade into a small saucepan. Scrape any clinging marinade ingredients off the steak into the saucepan. Bring the liquid to a boil and cook it for two minutes. Set it aside.

Pat the steak dry with paper towels and broil it for four minutes on the first side. Sprinkle the steak with the salt, turn the steak over and broil it about four minutes longer for medium-rare meat.

Let the steak rest at room temperature for 30 minutes, then slice it into thin strips. Cut each strip into 2-inch lengths. Add the beef, the cooled potatoes and the tomatoes to the beans.

Strain the marinade into a small bowl, discarding the solids left in the sieve. Whisk the oil and the mustard into the bowl to make a vinaigrette. Pour the vinaigrette over the salad and toss well. Refrigerate the salad for 20 minutes before serving it.

Grilled Beef and Fresh Salsa in Flour Tortillas

Serves 4
Working (and total) time: about 1 hour

Calories **375**
Protein **27g.**
Cholesterol **61mg.**
Total fat **10g.**
Saturated fat **2g.**
Sodium **185mg.**

1 lb. bottom round steak, trimmed of fat
2 tbsp. fresh lime juice
2 tbsp. tequila or gin
½ tsp. chili powder
½ tsp. dried oregano
¼ tsp. ground cumin
freshly ground black pepper
8 scallions, the green tops trimmed to 3 inches in length
8 flour tortillas, 10 inches in diameter
2 cups shredded romaine lettuce

Salsa

1 lb. ripe tomatoes, preferably plum tomatoes, peeled, seeded and finely chopped
1 green pepper, seeded, deribbed and finely diced
1 small onion, finely chopped
1 to 3 jalapeño peppers, seeded and finely chopped (caution, page 23)
2 tbsp. fresh lime juice
2 tbsp. chopped fresh cilantro
¼ tsp. salt

Slice the steak against the grain into ½-inch-wide strips. In a large, shallow dish, combine the lime juice, tequila or gin, chili powder, oregano, cumin and black pepper. Add the steak strips and the scallions, and toss them well. Let the steak marinate at room temperature for 20 minutes.

Combine the salsa ingredients in a bowl; let the salsa stand for at least 15 minutes to blend the flavors.

If you plan to grill the meat, prepare the coals in an outdoor grill about 30 minutes before cooking time; to broil, preheat the broiler for about 10 minutes.

Stack the tortillas and wrap them in aluminum foil.

Warm the tortillas in a preheated 350° F. oven for 10 minutes. Meanwhile, cook the steak strips in the center of the grill or broiler, with the scallions laid carefully at the side, for one minute per side; the steak should be medium rare and the scallions lightly charred. Cut the steak strips into pieces about 1 inch long.

To serve, place equal amounts of steak pieces and their juices on the tortillas. Add some lettuce and a scallion to each tortilla, then spoon some of the salsa over the top. Roll up the tortillas and serve them at once; pass any remaining salsa separately.

SUGGESTED ACCOMPANIMENT: *black beans and rice.*

Chilies — A Cautionary Note

Both dried and fresh hot chilies should be handled with care. Their flesh and seeds contain volatile oils that can make skin tingle and cause eyes to burn. Rubber gloves offer protection — but the cook should still be careful not to touch the face, lips or eyes when working with chilies.

Soaking fresh chilies in cold, salted water for an hour will remove some of their fire. If canned chilies are substituted for fresh ones, they should be rinsed in cold water in order to eliminate as much of the brine used to preserve them as possible.

Sirloin and Leek Kebabs

Serves 4
Working (and total) time: about 1 hour

Calories **335**
Protein **28g.**
Cholesterol **76mg.**
Total fat **7g.**
Saturated fat **3g.**
Sodium **210mg.**

1¼ lb. boneless sirloin steak, trimmed of fat and cut into long, thin, ½-inch-wide strips
½ tsp. ground white pepper
1 tsp. cayenne pepper
½ tsp. ground allspice
½ tsp. ground cumin
½ tsp. turmeric
¼ tsp. salt
3 leeks, washed thoroughly to remove all grit, white parts cut into ½-inch-wide strips, green parts reserved for another use
Ginger chutney
½ cup golden raisins
one 2-inch piece fresh ginger, peeled and chopped
½ small onion, chopped
1 tart apple, cored and quartered
½ cup fresh lime juice
1 tbsp. honey
¼ tsp. whole mustard seed

To make the chutney, chop the raisins, ginger, onion, apple, lime juice, honey and mustard seed in a food processor or a blender. Transfer the chutney to a bowl and refrigerate it.

If you plan to grill the kebabs, prepare the coals about 30 minutes before cooking time; to broil, preheat the broiler for about 10 minutes.

Combine the white pepper, cayenne pepper, allspice, cumin, turmeric and salt in a small bowl. Spread the strips of beef on a baking sheet or tray. With your fingers, rub the spice mixture into the beef. Set the beef aside.

Blanch the leeks in a large saucepan of boiling water for two minutes. Drain them and refresh them under cold running water, then drain them again.

Lay a strip of leek on top of each piece of meat.

Divide the meat and leeks among 12 skewers, threading the skewer through both leek and meat at frequent intervals.

Grill or broil the kebabs for one minute on each side for medium-rare meat, and serve them with the ginger chutney.

SUGGESTED ACCOMPANIMENT: *steamed rice tossed with peas.*

Grilled Sirloin Stuffed with Summer Vegetables

Serves 8
Working time: about 1 hour
Total time: about 2 hours (includes marinating)

Calories **210**
Protein **27g.**
Cholesterol **76mg.**
Total fat **9g.**
Saturated fat **3g.**
Sodium **190mg.**

one 2½-lb. sirloin steak, about 2 inches thick, trimmed of fat
1 tsp. Dijon mustard
¼ tsp. freshly ground black pepper
1 garlic clove, crushed
⅛ tsp. salt
¼ cup red wine
Vegetable stuffing
1 tbsp. olive oil
⅓ cup chopped onion
1 green pepper, seeded, deribbed and diced
1 sweet red pepper, seeded, deribbed and diced
¼ cup diced zucchini
¼ cup diced yellow squash
2 garlic cloves, finely chopped
1½ tsp. fresh thyme, or ½ tsp. dried thyme leaves
1½ tsp. chopped fresh oregano, or ½ tsp. dried oregano
¼ tsp. hot red-pepper flakes
¼ tsp. salt
freshly ground black pepper
¾ cup fresh bread crumbs

Using the technique shown at right, cut a pocket in the beef. Combine the mustard, pepper, garlic, salt and wine in a shallow dish. Add the steak to the dish and turn the meat in the marinade once to coat it evenly. Marinate the steak for one hour at room temperature or about three hours in the refrigerator, turning it several times.

Meanwhile, make the stuffing. Heat the oil in a large heavy-bottomed skillet over low heat. Add the onion, green and red pepper, zucchini, yellow squash and garlic. Partially cover the skillet and cook the vegetables, stirring frequently, until they begin to soften — about seven minutes. Add the thyme, oregano, red-pepper flakes, salt and some black pepper. Stir the mixture well and remove it from the heat. Add the bread crumbs and toss them with the vegetables. Allow the mixture to cool.

About 30 minutes before cooking the meat, prepare the coals for grilling. When the coals are nearly ready, remove the meat from the dish, reserving the mari-

nade. Stuff the beef with the cooled vegetable mixture and tie it as demonstrated below.

When the coals are hot, bank them against the sides of the grill. Place a foil drip pan in the center of the coal grate and set the rack in place. Lay the meat in the center of the rack. Grill the meat, basting it occasionally with the reserved marinade, for 20 minutes. Turn the meat over and continue cooking it for 10 to 20 minutes longer for medium-rare meat.

Remove the meat from the grill and let it stand for 30 minutes. Discard the strings and slice the meat across the grain. Arrange the slices on a platter and serve immediately. This dish can also be prepared ahead of time and served cold.

SUGGESTED ACCOMPANIMENTS: *grilled sliced potatoes; spinach salad.*

Cutting and Stuffing a Pocket in a Sirloin Steak

1 *CUTTING A POCKET. Insert the tip of a knife (here, a boning knife) into the side of a two-inch-thick boneless sirloin steak. Cut in as deeply as possible without piercing the outer edge of the meat to form a pocket.*

2 *STUFFING THE POCKET. Use your fingers to stuff the prepared filling (recipe, page 24) into the pocket. Be sure to push the filling in deep.*

3 *MAKING THE FIRST LOOP. To keep the pocket from opening during cooking, tie the piece as you would a roast. First, loop butcher's twine around one end of the steak and knot the string, leaving several inches of twine loose at that end.*

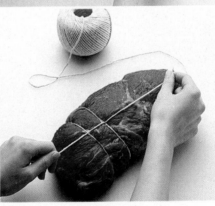

4 *MAKING SUCCESSIVE LOOPS. With the string still attached to the ball of twine, form a loose loop and twist it around twice. Bring the loop over and under the other end of the meat.*

5 *TIGHTENING THE STRING. Slide the loop forward so that it rests about 1½ to 2 inches in front of the first loop, and tighten it by pulling both ends of the twine at once. Repeat the process, making three or more loops around the meat and tightening the string after each loop.*

6 *TYING THE ROAST TOGETHER. Finally, draw the string under the entire length of the meat and back to the first loop you made. Knot the string to the loose length at that end, then sever the string from the ball of twine.*

Tournedos with Pepper Sauces

Serves 4
Working time: about 1 hour
Total time: about 2 hours and 15 minutes
(includes marinating)

Calories **280**
Protein **26g.**
Cholesterol **73mg.**
Total fat **12g.**
Saturated fat **4g.**
Sodium **190mg.**

one 1¼-lb. beef tenderloin roast, trimmed of fat and cut into 8 small steaks
1 garlic clove, finely chopped
1 cup red wine
½ cup fresh rosemary sprigs, or 1½ tbsp. dried rosemary
3 yellow or green peppers
3 sweet red peppers
2 tsp. red wine vinegar
¼ tsp. salt
one 1-lb. eggplant, sliced into 8 rounds
1 tbsp. olive oil
8 fresh rosemary sprigs for garnish (optional)

Put the steaks into a shallow dish large enough to hold them in a single layer. Sprinkle the garlic, wine and rosemary over the steaks and set them aside to marinate at room temperature for two hours.

About one hour before the steaks finish marinating, cook the peppers under a preheated broiler, turning them frequently until their skins blister — about eight minutes. Transfer the peppers to a large bowl and cover the bowl with plastic wrap — the trapped steam will loosen the skins. When the peppers are cool enough to handle, peel, seed and derib them over a sieve set in a bowl to catch the juices. Cut one of the yellow or green peppers and one of the red peppers into ¼-inch dice; reserve the dice for garnish.

Purée the remaining two yellow or green peppers in a blender or a food processor. Add to the purée 1 teaspoon of the vinegar, ⅛ teaspoon of the salt and half of the accumulated pepper juices. Pour the purée into a small saucepan and set it aside.

Purée the remaining two red peppers in the blender or food processor; add the remaining teaspoon of vinegar, the other ⅛ teaspoon of salt and the rest of the pepper juices, and pour this purée into a second small saucepan. Warm both sauces over medium-low heat while you prepare the eggplant and steaks.

With a paring knife, score both sides of each eggplant slice in a crosshatch pattern. Lightly brush both sides with the oil, then broil the slices until they are soft and browned — two to three minutes per side. Remove the slices from the broiler and keep them warm.

Take the steaks out of the marinade and pat them dry; discard the marinade. Broil the steaks until they are medium rare — about three minutes per side.

Place two eggplant slices on each of four dinner plates. Set a steak on each eggplant slice and spoon the warmed pepper sauces around the steaks. Garnish each portion with the reserved diced peppers — and, if you are using it, a sprig of fresh rosemary — just before serving.

SUGGESTED ACCOMPANIMENT: *sourdough bread.*

Beef Tenderloin Steaks Stuffed with Oysters, and Topped with Kale

THIS NEW DISH CALLS TO MIND AN OLD ONE POPULAR AT THE TURN OF THE CENTURY, BEEFSTEAK WITH OYSTER BLANKET, IN WHICH THE OYSTERS WERE SERVED ON TOP OF THE MEAT.

Serves 6
Working (and total time): about 1 hour

Calories **185**
Protein **23g.**
Cholesterol **77mg.**
Total fat **6g.**
Saturated fat **2g.**
Sodium **195mg.**

6 tenderloin steaks (about 4 oz. each), trimmed of fat
12 shucked oysters, with their liquid
6 shallots, finely chopped
3 tbsp. Champagne vinegar or red wine vinegar
¼ cup unsalted brown stock or unsalted chicken stock (recipes, page 137)
3 cups coarsely shredded, tightly packed kale
¼ tsp. salt
freshly ground black pepper

If you plan to grill the steaks, prepare the coals about 30 minutes before cooking time; to broil, preheat the broiler for about 10 minutes.

Poach the oysters in their liquid in a small saucepan over medium heat just until their edges curl — about one minute. With a slotted spoon, remove the oysters from the pan and set them aside. Strain the poaching ▶

liquid and reserve it.

Cut a slit in the side of each steak to make a pocket large enough to hold one of the oysters. Stuff the steaks with six of the oysters.

Cook the steaks on the grill or under the broiler for two to three minutes on each side for medium-rare steaks. Set the steaks aside in a warm place.

Heat the shallots, vinegar and stock in a large heavy-bottomed skillet over medium-high heat until the liq-uid boils. Continue cooking the mixture until it has reduced by one third — three to four minutes. Stir in the kale, the remaining oysters, the poaching liquid, the salt and some pepper. Toss the mixture until the greens begin to wilt — about two minutes.

Spoon the kale and oysters over the steaks and serve immediately.

SUGGESTED ACCOMPANIMENT: *baked potatoes.*

Skewered Beef with Julienned Papaya

Serves 8 as a main course or 16 as an appetizer
Working time: about 35 minutes
Total time: about 1 hour and 35 minutes
(includes marinating)

Calories **265**
Protein **25g.**
Cholesterol **54mg.**
Total fat **10g.**
Saturated fat **3g.**
Sodium **280mg.**

2 lb. top round steak, trimmed of fat
2 underripe papayas, or 4 mangoes, peeled, halved, seeded and julienned
2 tbsp. fresh lime juice
32 cherry tomatoes, halved lengthwise
2 scallions, green parts only, thinly sliced
2 tbsp. crushed unsalted roasted peanuts
Spicy peanut marinade
2½ tbsp. low-sodium soy sauce
2 scallions, white parts only, thinly sliced
1½ tbsp. finely chopped fresh ginger
3 garlic cloves, finely chopped
2 small dried red chili peppers, chopped (caution, page 23), or ¼ tsp. hot red-pepper flakes
3 tbsp. peanut butter
¼ cup plain low-fat yogurt
2 tbsp. dry white wine
2 tbsp. fresh lime juice
1 tbsp. honey

To make the marinade, combine the soy sauce with the scallions, ginger, garlic, and chili peppers or pepper flakes in a large bowl. Let the mixture stand for one minute, then whisk in the peanut butter, yogurt, wine, lime juice and honey.

Slice the beef into strips about 5 inches long and ⅛ inch thick — you will need at least 32 slices. Toss the meat in the marinade and allow it to sit for one hour at room temperature.

While the beef is marinating, combine the papaya or mango julienne and the lime juice in a bowl. Refrigerate the fruit mixture.

If you plan to grill the beef, prepare the coals in an outdoor grill about 30 minutes before cooking time; to broil, preheat the broiler for 10 minutes.

Insert a wooden skewer through a tomato half, then thread it through a strip of beef; finish with another tomato half. Repeat the process for the remaining to-matoes and beef. Brush the skewered meat and toma-toes with any remaining marinade.

Cook the meat in two batches until it begins to brown — four to six minutes. (Because the slices are so thin, the beef need be cooked on only one side.) Trans-fer the skewers to a serving platter.

Sprinkle the meat with the scallion greens and pea-nuts, and serve the chilled papaya or mango alongside.

SUGGESTED ACCOMPANIMENT: *roasted peppers.*

Roulades Stuffed with Watercress and Walnuts

Serves 8
Working (and total) time: about 40 minutes

Calories **190**
Protein **22g.**
Cholesterol **61mg.**
Total fat **11g.**
Saturated fat **2g.**
Sodium **145mg.**

one 2-lb. bottom round steak, about 1 inch thick, trimmed of fat
2 bunches watercress, washed and stemmed
1 lb. fresh spinach, washed and stemmed
1 tbsp. olive oil
¼ cup finely chopped walnuts
1 tbsp. finely chopped fresh rosemary, or 1½ tsp. dried rosemary
2 anchovies, rinsed, patted dry and finely chopped
¼ tsp. salt
freshly ground black pepper

Cut the steak in half across its width. Then, holding your knife blade parallel to the work surface, slice through both halves horizontally to form eight ¼-inch-thick slices. (Alternatively, ask the butcher to slice the meat for you.)

Place a slice of beef between two sheets of plastic wrap and flatten it to ⅛-inch thickness by pounding first one side and then the other with a meat mallet or the flat of a heavy knife. Flatten the remaining seven pieces in the same manner. Set the beef aside while you prepare the stuffing.

Bring 2 quarts of water to a boil in a large pot. Plunge the watercress into the boiling water and cook it for 30 seconds. Add the spinach, stir well, and cook the greens for 15 seconds longer. Drain the spinach and watercress, and squeeze them firmly into a ball to extract as much moisture as possible. Finely chop the ball of greens.

Heat ½ tablespoon of the oil in a heavy-bottomed skillet over medium heat. Add the walnuts, rosemary and anchovies. Cook the mixture, stirring, for one minute. Stir in the greens, salt and some pepper. Remove the skillet from the heat.

Preheat the oven to 425° F. Spread 2 tablespoons of the stuffing on each piece of meat, leaving a ¼-inch border around the edges. Roll up the pieces, starting at a long edge, and set the roulades seam side down on a broiler pan at least 1 inch apart.

Brush the roulades with the remaining ½ table-spoon of the oil. Bake them for 15 minutes. Remove the pan from the oven and allow the meat to stand for five minutes. Cut each roulade on the diagonal into six to eight thin slices.

SUGGESTED ACCOMPANIMENT: *steamed baby turnips.*

Beef Tenderloin and Potato Roast

Serves 4
Working time: about 20 minutes
Total time: about 1 hour and 10 minutes

Calories **290**
Protein **27g.**
Cholesterol **73mg.**
Total fat **9g.**
Saturated fat **3g.**
Sodium **145mg.**

one 1¼-lb. beef tenderloin roast, trimmed of fat and cut into 8 slices
½ tsp. ground allspice
¼ cup chopped parsley
1 tbsp. red wine vinegar
⅛ tsp. salt
1 lb. baking potatoes, scrubbed and cut into ¼-inch-thick slices
2 onions, thinly sliced
½ cup unsalted brown stock or unsalted chicken stock (recipes, page 137)

Preheat the oven to 350° F.

Mix the allspice, 2 tablespoons of the parsley, the vinegar and the salt in a small bowl. With your fingers, rub this mixture into the beef pieces and place them in a shallow dish. Let the meat marinate at room temperature while you make the potato gratin.

Combine the potatoes and onions in a flameproof baking dish. Pour in the stock and 1 cup of water. Bring the liquid to a boil over medium-high heat, then bake the potatoes in the oven until they are tender and have browned — about 45 minutes. (If you do not have a flameproof baking dish, bring the potatoes, onions, stock and water to a boil in a saucepan, then transfer the mixture to a baking dish, and proceed as above.)

When the potatoes are cooked, remove the dish from the oven and increase the temperature to 450° F.

Heat a nonstick skillet over medium-high heat. Pat the beef slices dry with a paper towel and sear them for 30 seconds on each side. Set the beef on top of the potatoes and return the dish to the oven. Bake the beef and potatoes for three minutes; turn the meat and bake it for three minutes more.

Sprinkle the remaining 2 tablespoons of parsley over the top before serving the roast.

SUGGESTED ACCOMPANIMENT: *steamed Brussels sprouts.*

Layered Meat Loaf

Serves 8
Working time: about 40 minutes
Total time: about 2 hours

Calories **220**
Protein **23g.**
Cholesterol **56mg.**
Total fat **8g.**
Saturated fat **3g.**
Sodium **230mg.**

1¾ lb. beef round, trimmed of fat and ground (box, page 8)
2 large, ripe tomatoes (about 1 lb.), peeled, seeded and chopped
1 onion, chopped
3 garlic cloves, finely chopped
1½ tsp. chopped fresh oregano, or ½ tsp. dried oregano
½ cup port or Madeira
2 tbsp. red wine vinegar
1 tbsp. sugar
¼ tsp. salt
freshly ground black pepper
6 tbsp. freshly grated Parmesan cheese
⅔ cup dry bread crumbs
1 egg white
1 tbsp. safflower oil
2 bunches watercress, trimmed and washed
1 tbsp. fresh thyme, or 1 tsp. dried thyme leaves

Heat a large, heavy-bottomed skillet over medium-high heat. Put in the tomatoes, onion, garlic and oregano. Cook the vegetables, stirring occasionally, for five minutes. Add the port or Madeira, vinegar, sugar, ⅛ teaspoon of the salt and some pepper. Cook the mixture until almost all of the liquid has evaporated —

about 10 minutes. Purée the mixture and place all but ¼ cup of it in a large bowl. Preheat the oven to 400° F.

Add the beef, 4 tablespoons of the grated cheese, ⅓ cup of the bread crumbs, the remaining ⅛ teaspoon of salt, some pepper and the egg white to the tomato mixture in the bowl. Mix the ingredients well and set the meat aside while you prepare the watercress.

Heat the oil in a large, heavy-bottomed skillet over high heat. Add the watercress, thyme, and some pepper. Cook, stirring constantly, until the watercress has wilted and almost all of the liquid has evaporated — three to four minutes. Chop the watercress finely. Place it in a bowl and combine it with the remaining ⅓ cup of bread crumbs.

To layer the meat loaf, divide the beef mixture into three equal portions. Using a rolling pin or your hands, flatten each portion into a rectangle 5 inches wide, 8 inches long and ¾ inch thick.

Place one rectangle in a shallow baking pan. Top it with half of the watercress mixture, spreading the watercress evenly over the surface. Lay another rectangle on top and cover it with the remaining watercress. Finish with the final rectangle, then spread the reserved tomato sauce over the top and sides of the loaf. Sprinkle on the remaining 2 tablespoons of Parmesan cheese and bake the meat loaf for one hour and 10 minutes. Let the meat loaf stand for 10 minutes, then carefully transfer it to a platter, slice it and serve.

SUGGESTED ACCOMPANIMENT: *boiled new potatoes.*

Rump Roast with Root Vegetables

Serves 8
Working time: about 20 minutes
Total time: about 2 hours

Calories **205**
Protein **24g.**
Cholesterol **60mg.**
Total fat **7g.**
Saturated fat **2g.**
Sodium **165mg.**

one 2¼-lb. rump roast, trimmed of fat
1 tsp. safflower oil
¼ tsp. salt
½ tsp. cracked black peppercorns
1 garlic clove, finely chopped
2 large carrots, peeled and sliced into ¾-inch-thick rounds
2 large turnips, peeled and cut into ½-inch-thick wedges
1 rutabaga, peeled and cut into ¾-inch cubes
½ lb. small white onions
½ tbsp. fresh thyme, or ¾ tsp. dried thyme leaves
4 tsp. cornstarch
¼ cup low-fat milk
2 tsp. grainy mustard

Preheat the oven to 325° F.

Heat a large, nonstick skillet over medium-high heat. Add the oil, tilting the pan to coat the bottom. Sear the roast in the pan — approximately one minute on each side.

Transfer the meat to a roasting pan, sprinkle the meat with the salt, peppercorns and garlic, and roast the beef until it is medium rare and registers 140° F. on a meat thermometer — about one hour and 15 minutes. Remove the roast from the pan and set it aside. Skim and discard any fat from the juices in the pan; set the pan with its juices aside.

Toss the carrots, turnips, rutabaga and onions with the thyme. Pour enough water into a large pot to fill it 1 inch deep. Place a vegetable steamer in the pot and bring the water to a boil. Put the vegetables into the steamer, cover the pot, and cook the vegetables until they are tender — about 10 minutes. Remove the vegetables from the steamer and keep them warm.

Pour about 1 cup of the steaming liquid into the roasting pan. Simmer the liquid over medium-high heat, stirring constantly to dissolve any caramelized roasting juices on the bottom of the pan. Mix the cornstarch and milk in a small bowl, then whisk this mixture into the simmering liquid. Stir the liquid until the sauce thickens, then whisk in the mustard. Remove the pan from the heat and keep it warm.

Slice the roast and arrange the slices on a platter. Toss the vegetables with some of the sauce and place them around the meat. Serve the roast with the remaining sauce passed separately.

SUGGESTED ACCOMPANIMENT: *steamed kale or spinach.*

Spicy Beef Salad

Serves 4
Working time: about 25 minutes
Total time: about 2 hours and 45 minutes
(includes marinating)

Calories **295**
Protein **22g.**
Cholesterol **57mg.**
Total fat **5g.**
Saturated fat **2g.**
Sodium **120mg.**

one 1-lb. boneless sirloin steak, trimmed of fat
8 whole cloves
8 black peppercorns
12 allspice berries
1 large onion, thinly sliced
2 tbsp. Cognac or other brandy
2 cups red wine
6 oz. mixed dried fruit, coarsely chopped
¼ cup red wine vinegar
1 cinnamon stick
1 lb. turnips, peeled, halved lengthwise and sliced
¼ cup chopped fresh parsley
several watercress sprigs (optional), trimmed, washed and dried

Put the steak into a shallow pan with the cloves, peppercorns, allspice berries, onion slices, brandy, and 1 cup of the wine. Let the steak marinate at room temperature for two hours, turning it every now and then.

In a saucepan, combine the dried fruit with the vinegar, the remaining cup of wine, 1 cup of water and the cinnamon stick. Bring the liquid to a boil, then lower the heat, and simmer the mixture for 30 minutes. Drain the fruit in a sieve set over a bowl; discard the cinnamon stick and set the fruit aside. Return the liquid to the saucepan and boil it until it is reduced by about half — approximately five minutes.

Preheat the oven to 475° F.

Pour enough water into a saucepan to fill it about 1 inch deep. Set a vegetable steamer in the pan and bring the water to a boil. Put the turnips into the steamer, cover the pan, and steam the turnips until they are tender — about 10 minutes. Transfer the turnips to a bowl and set them aside.

Remove the steak from the marinade and pat it dry with paper towels; discard the marinade. Roast the steak for 15 minutes, then remove it from the oven, and let it rest for 30 minutes. Cut the steak against the grain into slices about ¼ inch thick. Cut each slice into strips about 1½ inches long.

Toss the strips of beef with the reduced wine mixture, parsley, turnips and the reserved fruit. Arrange the salad on a platter; garnish it with watercress, if you like, and serve.

SUGGESTED ACCOMPANIMENT: *small whole-wheat dinner rolls.*

Skewered Meatballs with Eggplant Relish

Serves 8
Working time: about 1 hour
Total time: about 1 hour and 30 minutes

Calories **235**
Protein **26g.**
Cholesterol **61mg.**
Total fat **7g.**
Saturated fat **2g.**
Sodium **190mg.**

2¼ lb. round, trimmed of fat and ground (box, page 8)
2 eggplants (about 2 lb.), pierced in several places with a knife
2 onions, finely chopped
6 garlic cloves, finely chopped
1 tsp. olive oil
4 tbsp. chopped fresh mint, or 2 tsp. dried oregano

3 tbsp. fresh lemon juice
¼ tsp. salt
freshly ground black pepper
4 slices whole-wheat bread
5 tbsp. chopped parsley
½ cup plain low-fat yogurt
several mint sprigs (optional)

Preheat the oven to 500° F.

Roast the eggplants in the oven, turning them occasionally, until they are blistered on all sides — about 20 minutes. Transfer the eggplants to a bowl, cover it with plastic wrap and refrigerate it.

Simmer the onion, garlic, oil and ¼ cup of water ▶

in a heavy-bottomed saucepan until the onion is translucent — about five minutes. Increase the heat and boil the mixture until the water has evaporated — approximately one minute.

To prepare the relish, peel the skin from the eggplants and purée the flesh in a blender or a food processor. Remove ¼ cup of the eggplant purée and set it aside. In a small bowl, combine the rest of the eggplant with the chopped mint or dried oregano, lemon juice, half of the onion and garlic mixture, ⅛ teaspoon of the salt and a generous grinding of pepper. Put the eggplant relish into the refrigerator.

Soak the bread slices for three minutes in enough water to cover them. Using your hands, gently squeeze the water from the bread.

Mix the ground beef, moist bread, parsley, the rest of the onion and garlic mixture, the reserved ¼ cup of the eggplant purée, the remaining ⅛ teaspoon of salt and a generous grinding of black pepper. Form the meat mixture into 48 meatballs. Thread three meatballs on each of 16 skewers and set them on a baking sheet. Cook the meatballs in the oven until they are browned — 10 to 15 minutes.

Arrange the meatballs on a platter and, if you like, garnish the dish with sprigs of mint. Pass the eggplant relish and the eggplant separately.

SUGGESTED ACCOMPANIMENT: *pita bread.*

Mediterranean Meat Loaf

Serves 10
Working time: about 1 hour
Total time: about 2 hours

Calories **220**
Protein **22g.**
Cholesterol **50mg.**
Total fat **6g.**
Saturated fat **2g.**
Sodium **140mg.**

2¼ lb. beef round, trimmed of fat and ground (box, page 8)
1 tsp. olive oil
2 carrots, finely chopped
2 celery stalks, finely chopped
2 onions, finely chopped
1 lb. eggplant, finely chopped
1 sweet red pepper, seeded, deribbed and finely chopped
1 green pepper, seeded, deribbed and finely chopped
8 garlic cloves, finely chopped
6 large ripe tomatoes, peeled, seeded and chopped, or 28 oz. canned unsalted whole tomatoes, crushed and drained
¼ cup finely chopped fresh oregano, or 4 tsp. dried oregano
3 cups fresh bread crumbs
2 tbsp. currants (optional)
20 canned grape leaves, stemmed, rinsed and patted dry (optional)

Heat a large, nonstick skillet over medium heat. Add the oil, carrots, celery, onions, eggplant, peppers and garlic. Cook the mixture, stirring frequently, until the vegetables are soft — about eight minutes.

Add the tomatoes and oregano to the skillet. Increase the heat to medium high and bring the liquid to a simmer, then simmer the tomatoes for two minutes. Remove half the mixture and set it aside.

Continue cooking the mixture remaining in the skillet until the liquid has evaporated — about 10 minutes. Scrape the vegetables into a large bowl and let them cool slightly. Add the beef, the bread crumbs and the currants, if you are using them. Knead the mixture with your hands to incorporate the ingredients.

Preheat the oven to 350° F.

Line a 3-quart ring mold with the grape leaves if you are using them — this adds a special effect. Spoon the meat mixture into the mold, patting it down to release trapped air. Trim any protruding grape leaves.

Bake the loaf for one hour. After about 50 minutes, reheat the reserved vegetable mixture over medium heat. Invert a serving plate on top of the mold; turn both over, then gently lift off the mold. Fill the space in the center of the meat loaf with some of the hot vegetables and spoon the rest into a bowl.

SUGGESTED ACCOMPANIMENT: *orzo or other small pasta.*

Beef Tenderloin Roast with Spinach Sauce and Almonds

Serves 6
Working time: about 20 minutes
Total time: about 1 hour

Calories **230**	one 1¾-lb. beef tenderloin roast, trimmed of fat
Protein **22g.**	
Cholesterol **64mg.**	4 tsp. safflower oil
Total fat **13g.**	¼ tsp. salt
Saturated fat **3g.**	freshly ground black pepper
Sodium **165mg.**	2 tbsp. slivered almonds
	3 tbsp. finely chopped shallot
	1 cup dry white wine
	½ lb. fresh spinach, stemmed and washed
	¼ cup skim milk
	⅛ tsp. grated nutmeg

Preheat the oven to 325° F.

Heat 1 teaspoon of the oil in a large, nonstick skillet over high heat. Sear the meat in the skillet until it is browned on all sides — two to three minutes in all. Season the tenderloin with ⅛ teaspoon of the salt and a liberal grinding of pepper. Transfer the tenderloin to a roasting pan; do not wash the skillet. Finish cooking the meat in the oven — about 35 minutes, or until a meat thermometer inserted in the center registers 140° F. for medium-rare meat.

Heat a small, heavy-bottomed skillet over medium heat. Add the slivered almonds and toast them, stirring constantly, until they are lightly browned — two to three minutes. Remove the toasted almonds from the skillet and set them aside.

To make the sauce, heat the remaining tablespoon of oil in the large skillet over medium heat. Add the shallot and cook it until it is translucent — about two minutes. Pour in the wine and simmer the liquid until about ⅓ cup remains — six to eight minutes.

Remove the roast from the oven and let it rest for 10 minutes while you complete the sauce.

Add the spinach to the shallot-wine mixture and reduce the heat to low. Cover the pan and cook the spinach until it has wilted — one or two minutes. Stir in the milk and nutmeg. Return the mixture to a simmer, then transfer it to a blender or a food processor, and purée it. Season the sauce with the remaining ⅛ teaspoon of salt and some pepper.

Carve the tenderloin into 12 slices and arrange them on a warmed serving platter. Spoon some of the sauce over the slices and sprinkle them with the almonds. Pass the remaining sauce separately.

SUGGESTED ACCOMPANIMENT: *steamed julienned carrots.*

Roast Eye Round with Mushroom Sauce

Serves 10
Working time: about 30 minutes
Total time: about 1 hour

Calories **205**
Protein **21g.**
Cholesterol **56mg.**
Total fat **10g.**
Saturated fat **3g.**
Sodium **170mg.**

one 2½-lb. eye round roast, trimmed of fat
¼ cup cracked black peppercorns
2½ tbsp. Dijon mustard
2 tbsp. plain low-fat yogurt
2 tbsp. olive oil
½ lb. mushrooms, wiped clean and quartered
⅓ cup thinly sliced shallots
1 tbsp. chopped fresh rosemary, or ¾ tsp. dried rosemary
1 cup red wine
1 garlic clove, finely chopped
2 cups unsalted brown stock or unsalted chicken stock, (recipes, page 137)
¼ tsp. salt
¼ cup heavy cream, mixed with 1 tbsp. cornstarch

Preheat the oven to 500° F.

Spread the cracked peppercorns on a plate. Mix 2 tablespoons of the mustard with the yogurt and smear this mixture over the beef. Roll the beef in the peppercorns, coating it evenly on all sides. Place the beef on a rack set in a roasting pan. For medium-rare meat, cook the roast until a meat thermometer inserted in the center registers 140° F. — about 35 minutes. Let the roast stand while you prepare the mushroom sauce.

Heat the oil in a large, heavy-bottomed skillet over medium heat. Add the mushrooms, shallots and rosemary, and cook them, stirring often, for five minutes. Add the wine and garlic, then rapidly boil the liquid until it is reduced by half — about three minutes. Stir in the stock and salt; reduce the sauce once again until only about 1¼ cups of liquid remain. Whisk in the cream-and-cornstarch mixture along with the remaining ½ tablespoon of mustard; simmer the sauce for one minute more to thicken it.

To serve, carve the roast into 20 very thin slices. Arrange the slices on a platter and pour the mushroom sauce over them.

SUGGESTED ACCOMPANIMENT: *steamed broccoli florets.*

Beef Tenderloin Roast with Spinach and Sprouts

Serves 8
Working time: about 30 minutes
Total time: about 2 hours (includes marinating)

Calories **240**
Protein **27g.**
Cholesterol **73mg.**
Total fat **12g.**
Saturated fat **4g.**
Sodium **160mg.**

one 2½-lb. beef tenderloin roast, trimmed of fat
2 tbsp. toasted sesame seeds
4 tbsp. low-sodium soy sauce
3 tbsp. rice vinegar or white wine vinegar
1 tbsp. dark brown sugar
1 tbsp. safflower oil
¾ lb. fresh spinach, washed, stemmed and sliced into ¼-inch-wide strips
2 large ripe tomatoes, peeled, seeded and sliced into ¼-inch-wide strips
4 cups bean sprouts

To make the marinade, purée 1 tablespoon of the sesame seeds, 3 tablespoons of the soy sauce, 2 tablespoons of the vinegar and the brown sugar in a blender. Put the tenderloin into a shallow dish, then pour the marinade over it, and let it stand for one hour at room temperature, turning the meat occasionally.

Preheat the oven to 325° F. Drain the tenderloin, discarding the marinade, and pat it dry with paper towels. Pour the oil into a large, ovenproof skillet set over high heat. When the oil is hot, sear the meat until it is well browned on all sides — three to five minutes. Place the skillet in the oven. For medium-rare meat, roast the tenderloin for 40 to 45 minutes or until a meat thermometer inserted in the center registers 140° F. Remove the meat from the oven and let it rest while you prepare the garnish.

Heat a large skillet or wok over medium heat. Add the spinach strips and cook them, stirring constantly, until their liquid has evaporated — two to three minutes. Stir in the tomatoes and sprouts, and cook the vegetables until they are heated through — three to four minutes more. Remove the pan from the heat and stir in the remaining tablespoon of soy sauce and the remaining tablespoon of vinegar.

Cut the tenderloin into 16 slices and arrange them on a platter. Surround the beef slices with the spinach-and-sprout garnish. Sprinkle the remaining tablespoon of sesame seeds over the garnish and serve.

SUGGESTED ACCOMPANIMENT: *boiled potatoes tossed with finely chopped scallion greens.*

Beef Tenderloin Filled with Basil and Sun-Dried Tomatoes

Serves 4
Working time: about 35 minutes
Total time: about 2 hours

Calories **340**
Protein **28g.**
Cholesterol **74mg.**
Total fat **17g.**
Saturated fat **4g.**
Sodium **415mg.**

one 1¼-lb. beef tenderloin roast, trimmed of fat	
1 cup loosely packed basil leaves, thinly sliced	
¼ cup sun-dried tomatoes packed in oil, drained and finely chopped	
1 tsp. safflower oil	

Stuffed cherry tomatoes

2 whole garlic bulbs, the cloves separated but not peeled
1 cup loosely packed fresh basil leaves
⅛ tsp. salt
freshly ground black pepper
1 tsp. fresh lemon juice
¼ cup plain low-fat yogurt
24 cherry tomatoes

Preheat the oven to 325° F.

Using a well-scrubbed sharpening steel or some other thick, pointed tool, pierce the tenderloin through the center; rotate the sharpening steel to create a ½-inch-wide hole.

Combine the thinly sliced basil leaves with the sun-dried tomatoes. Using your fingers, fill the tenderloin with the basil-tomato mixture.

Heat the oil in a heavy-bottomed, ovenproof skillet

over high heat. When the oil is hot, sear the roast until it is well browned on all sides — three to five minutes. Transfer the skillet to the oven. For medium-rare meat, roast the tenderloin for 25 to 30 minutes or until a thermometer inserted in the meat registers 140° F. Remove the tenderloin from the oven and let it rest until it is cool — about 45 minutes.

Meanwhile, prepare the filling for the cherry tomatoes. Put the garlic cloves into a small saucepan and pour in just enough water to cover them. Bring the water to a boil, then reduce the heat, and simmer the cloves until they are very soft — 30 to 45 minutes. Drain the garlic; when the cloves are cool enough to handle, squeeze the pulp from the skins into a blender or a food processor. Add the unsliced basil leaves, the salt, some pepper, the lemon juice and the yogurt, and purée the mixture. Set the purée aside.

Cut the tops off the cherry tomatoes. With a melon baller or a small spoon, scoop out the seeds. Using a piping bag or a spoon, fill the tomatoes with the purée.

Carve the tenderloin into ¼-inch-thick slices and transfer them to plates or a platter. Arrange the filled tomatoes around the slices of tenderloin and serve the meat at room temperature.

SUGGESTED ACCOMPANIMENT: *whole-wheat dinner rolls.*

Roast Beef with Cloves and Red Peppers

Serves 12
Working time: about 30 minutes
Total time: about 2 hours

Calories **180**
Protein **23g.**
Cholesterol **63mg.**
Total fat **7g.**
Saturated fat **2g.**
Sodium **155mg.**

one 3½-lb. tip roast, trimmed of fat
4 sweet red peppers
1 tsp. ground cloves
1 tbsp. safflower oil
½ tsp. salt
freshly ground black pepper
1 cup unsalted brown stock or unsalted chicken stock (recipes, page 137)
2 white onions (about 1 lb.)
½ cup dry white wine

Roast the peppers about 2 inches below a preheated broiler, turning them as they blister, until they are blackened on all sides — about 15 minutes in all. Transfer the peppers to a bowl and cover it with plastic wrap; the trapped steam will loosen their skins. Set the bowl aside.

Preheat the oven to 275° F. Sprinkle the meat all over with ½ teaspoon of the cloves.

Heat the oil in a large, heavy-bottomed skillet over high heat. When it is hot, add the beef and sear it until it is well browned on all sides — about five minutes. Transfer the beef to a shallow, flameproof casserole and sprinkle it with ¼ teaspoon of the salt and a generous grinding of pepper.

Roast the beef for one hour. If the meat juices begin to blacken in the bottom of the casserole, pour in a few tablespoons of the stock.

While the roast is cooking, peel the peppers, working over a bowl to catch the juice. Strain the juice and set it aside. Slice the peppers into strips about 1 inch long and ½ inch wide. Cut the onions in half from top to bottom, then slice them with the grain into strips roughly the same size as the pepper strips.

When the roast has cooked for one hour, add to the casserole the peppers and their juice, the onions, the stock, the wine, the remaining ½ teaspoon of cloves and the remaining ¼ teaspoon of salt. For medium-rare meat, roast the beef for 30 minutes longer, or until a meat thermometer inserted into the center registers 140°F.

Remove the casserole from the oven and set the roast aside while you finish the dish.

With a slotted spoon, transfer the vegetables to a bowl. Boil the liquid remaining in the casserole until it is reduced to about ½ cup. Cut the meat into very thin slices and arrange them on a platter with the vegetables surrounding them. Drizzle the sauce over the beef and serve immediately.

SUGGESTED ACCOMPANIMENT: *roasted sweet potatoes.*

Mushroom-Stuffed
Top Loin Roast

Serves 8
Working time: about 45 minutes
Total time: about 2 hours

Calories **190**
Protein **26g.**
Cholesterol **65mg.**
Total fat **7g.**
Saturated fat **3g.**
Sodium **200mg.**

one 2½-lb. top loin roast, trimmed of fat	
½ lb. fresh shiitake mushrooms, wiped clean, caps finely chopped, stems reserved	
½ lb. mushrooms, wiped clean, caps finely chopped, stems reserved	

2½ cups dry white wine

½ cup Madeira or port

8 scallions, white parts finely chopped,
green parts reserved

grated zest of 3 lemons

½ tsp. salt

freshly ground black pepper

¼ cup toasted bread crumbs

Preheat the oven to 400° F.

Combine the mushrooms, 2 cups of the white wine,
and the Madeira or port in a large, nonreactive skillet.
Bring the liquid to a boil over medium-high heat, then

continue cooking it until all the liquid has evaporated — about 15 minutes. Transfer the mushrooms to a bowl and mix in the chopped scallions, lemon zest, salt and some pepper. Set the mixture aside.

Using the techniques shown below, cut the roast and stuff it. Put the roast into a roasting pan and cover the exposed mushroom mixture with the bread crumbs. Scatter the reserved mushroom stems and scallions around the meat and roast it for 30 minutes.

Pour the remaining ½ cup of white wine over the roast and continue roasting the beef for 15 minutes for medium-rare meat. (The internal temperature should be 140° F.) Transfer the roast to a cutting board and allow it to rest for 15 minutes.

Heat the juices in the roasting pan over medium heat, scraping up any caramelized juices with a wooden spoon to dissolve them. Skim off the fat, strain the juices and keep them warm.

Carve the roast into eight slices and serve them with the juices spooned on top.

SUGGESTED ACCOMPANIMENT: *steamed spinach.*
EDITOR'S NOTE: *If fresh shiitake mushrooms are unavailable in your market, regular mushrooms may be substituted.*

Stuffing a Top Loin Roast

1 *TRIMMING THE FAT IN STRIPS. With a small, thin-bladed knife (here, a boning knife), cut into the fatty layer of the loin roast to form a tab. Pull the tab taut, and insert the knife under it. Carefully slide the knife toward you to remove a strip of fat. Continue cutting off strips until the entire layer of fat is removed.*

2 *MAKING THE FIRST SLICE. Steadying the roast with one hand, place a slicing knife along the meat's edge, about one third of the way down from the surface. With a smooth sawing motion, cut across the meat, stopping just short of the edge so that the flaps remain attached.*

3 *MAKING THE SECOND SLICE. Rotate the meat on the work surface and unfold the thinner flap from the thicker one. Now cut through the inside edge of the thicker flap, again leaving a small hinge of meat to keep the pieces connected.*

4 *STUFFING THE LOIN. Unfold the newly formed flap. You will have three joined squares of meat. Spread one third of the stuffing onto the middle square and fold the left flap over it. Spread half of the remaining stuffing on top (above). Fold the right flap over the stuffing and cover the flap with the rest of the stuffing.*

Beef and Wheat-Berry Salad

Serves 6
Working time: about 25 minutes
Total time: about 45 minutes

Calories **355**
Protein **29g.**
Cholesterol **63mg.**
Total fat **10g.**
Saturated fat **3g.**
Sodium **235mg.**

1½ lb. boneless sirloin steak, trimmed of fat and cut into strips about 1½ inches long and ⅛ inch thick
1½ cups wheat berries, rinsed
½ tsp. salt
2 leeks, trimmed, or 2 bunches scallions, trimmed
1 tbsp. olive oil
2 tsp. fresh thyme, or ¾ tsp. dried thyme leaves
8 large radishes, quartered
¼ cup cider vinegar
1½ tbsp. fresh lemon juice
freshly ground black pepper

Bring 2½ cups of water to a boil in a saucepan. Add the wheat berries and ¼ teaspoon of the salt. Reduce the heat to low and cover the pan with the lid ajar. Simmer the wheat berries until they are just tender — about 45 minutes. Drain the wheat berries and set them aside.

Meanwhile, if you are using leeks, slice them into rounds about ½ inch wide. Wash the rounds in two or three changes of cold water to rid them of grit. Drain the rounds and set them aside. (If you are using the scallions, simply slice them.)

Ten minutes before the wheat berries are ready, heat 2 teaspoons of the oil in a large, nonstick skillet over high heat. Add the beef and thyme, and cook them, stirring frequently, for two minutes; transfer the beef to a large bowl.

Return the skillet to the heat and add the remaining teaspoon of oil. Add the leeks or scallions and the radishes, and cook them, stirring frequently, for three minutes. Pour in the vinegar, lemon juice, the reserved beef and wheat berries, the remaining ¼ teaspoon of salt, and a generous grinding of black pepper. Continue cooking, stirring frequently, for one additional minute. With a slotted spoon, transfer the mixture to a large serving bowl.

Return the skillet to high heat and boil the liquid until it is reduced to ¼ cup. Pour the reduced liquid over the salad and toss well. Serve the salad warm or chilled.

SUGGESTED ACCOMPANIMENTS: *sliced fruit; French bread.*

Beef Tenderloin Stir Fried with Butternut Squash and Turnips

Serves 4
Working time: about 15 minutes
Total time: about 25 minutes

Calories **215**
Protein **20g.**
Cholesterol **54mg.**
Total fat **10g.**
Saturated fat **3g.**
Sodium **235mg.**

1 lb. beef tenderloin, trimmed of fat and sliced into 2-inch-long strips
1¼ cups unsalted brown stock or unsalted chicken stock (recipes, page 137)
1 small onion, thinly sliced
2 turnips (about ½ lb.), peeled, quartered and cut into ¼-inch-thick slices
½ small butternut squash (about ¾ lb.), peeled, quartered and cut into ¼-inch-thick slices
2 tbsp. chopped fresh tarragon, or 2 tsp. dried tarragon
¼ tsp. salt
freshly ground black pepper
1 tbsp. safflower oil
1 garlic clove, finely chopped
1 tbsp. cornstarch, mixed with 1 tbsp. water
1 tsp. distilled white vinegar

Place the stock and the onion in a saucepan. Set a vegetable steamer in the pan and bring the stock to a simmer. In the meantime, sprinkle the turnips and the squash separately with 1 tablespoon of the fresh tarragon or all of the dried. Put the turnips into the steamer, cover it, and steam the turnips for two minutes. Add the squash and continue steaming the vegetables until they are tender — about three minutes. Transfer the vegetables to a plate and set them aside; remove the steamer from the saucepan and reserve the stock and onion.

Season the beef with the salt and pepper. Heat ½ tablespoon of the oil in a well-seasoned wok or a heavy-bottomed skillet over high heat, and sear the beef, tossing continuously to prevent it from sticking, for about two minutes. Turn off the heat, transfer the meat to a plate, and keep it warm. Wipe out the wok or skillet with a paper towel and set it over high heat again. Add the remaining ½ tablespoon of oil, the garlic and the reserved vegetables, and cook them briefly, stirring continuously, for three minutes. Add the beef, toss well, and push the ingredients to the sides of the wok or skillet. Pour in the reserved stock and onions and bring them to a simmer. Whisk in the cornstarch mixture and the vinegar, whisking continuously until the liquid thickens — about two minutes. Serve the beef and vegetables with the sauce. If you are using fresh tarragon, sprinkle the remaining tablespoon over the top.

SUGGESTED ACCOMPANIMENT: *rice tossed with chives.*

Top Round Steak with Mushrooms and Red Onions

Serves 8
Working time: about 1 hour
Total time: about 3 hours (includes marinating time)

Calories **245**
Protein **29g.**
Cholesterol **72mg.**
Total fat **8g.**
Saturated fat **3g.**
Sodium **70mg.**

one 2½-lb. top round steak, trimmed of fat
2 red onions, cut into ½-inch-thick slices
1½ cups red wine
¼ cup raspberry vinegar or distilled white vinegar
¼ cup fresh lime juice
20 juniper berries
1 lb. fresh mushrooms, wiped clean
¾ cup unsalted brown stock or unsalted chicken stock (recipes, page 137)
2 tbsp. cornstarch
freshly ground black pepper
¼ cup finely chopped fresh parsley

Spread the onion slices in the bottom of a shallow baking dish. Set the steak on the onions; pour the wine, vinegar and lime juice over the steak, then scatter the juniper berries over all. Let the steak marinate at room temperature for two hours or put it into the refrigerator overnight.

Remove the steak and onions from the marinade, and pat them dry with paper towels. Strain the marinade into a bowl and set it aside. Discard the berries.

Heat a large, nonstick skillet over high heat. Add the onion slices and sauté them until they are tender — about four minutes on each side. Remove them from the skillet and keep them warm. Cook the steak in the skillet over medium-high heat for four minutes on each side for medium-rare meat. Remove the steak from the skillet and let it rest while you prepare the mushrooms.

Sauté the mushrooms in the skillet over high heat, stirring occasionally, until most of the juices have evaporated — about five minutes. Remove the mushrooms with a slotted spoon and set them aside. Pour the steak marinade into the skillet and boil it until it has reduced by half — about 10 minutes. Mix the stock and the cornstarch together and whisk them into the reduced marinade. Bring the liquid to a boil and continue cooking until it thickens slightly — about one minute. Season the mushrooms with some black pepper and stir them, along with the parsley, into the sauce.

Slice the steak and arrange it on a serving platter with the onions. Spoon the mushrooms around the steak just before serving.

SUGGESTED ACCOMPANIMENT: *French bread.*

Southeast-Asian Beef Noodles

Serves 4
Working (and total) time: about 45 minutes

Calories **420**
Protein **33g.**
Cholesterol **72mg.**
Total fat **13g.**
Saturated fat **3g.**
Sodium **260mg.**

1¼ lb. top round, trimmed of fat and cut into paper-thin slices
1 tbsp. low-sodium soy sauce
2 tbsp. dry sherry or dry white wine
2 tbsp. sugar
freshly ground black pepper
1½ tbsp. cornstarch
6 oz. fresh Asian wheat noodles, or ¼ lb. vermicelli
4 tsp. safflower oil

1 small onion, halved and sliced lengthwise
1 carrot, peeled, halved lengthwise and thinly sliced on the diagonal
½ lb. broccoli stems, peeled, halved lengthwise and thinly sliced on the diagonal
½ sweet red pepper, seeded, deribbed and cut into narrow strips about 2 inches long
2 tsp. finely chopped fresh ginger
4 garlic cloves, finely chopped
1 cup unsalted brown stock or unsalted chicken stock (recipes, page 137)
½ tbsp. sweet chili sauce, or ½ tsp. hot red-pepper flakes mixed with ½ tsp. corn syrup and ½ tsp. rice vinegar
1 tbsp. fresh lemon juice
1 tbsp. hoisin sauce or low-sodium soy sauce

In a large bowl, combine the beef slices with the tablespoon of soy sauce, the sherry or white wine, 1 tablespoon of the sugar, some pepper and ½ tablespoon of the cornstarch. Set the mixture aside.

Put the noodles or vermicelli into 3 quarts of boiling water. Start testing the noodles after three minutes and cook them until they are *al dente*. (If you are using vermicelli, start testing them after seven minutes.) Drain the pasta in a colander and rinse it under very hot water. Drain the pasta again and transfer it to a serving platter. Cover the platter with aluminum foil to keep the pasta warm.

Heat 2 teaspoons of the oil in a large, nonstick skillet or well-seasoned wok over high heat. Add the onion slices and stir fry them for one minute. Add the carrot and broccoli, and stir fry them for one minute. Mix in the red pepper and stir fry the mixture for two minutes more. Mound the vegetables on top of the pasta, then cover the platter with the foil once more, and keep it warm.

Heat the remaining 2 teaspoons of oil in the skillet over high heat. Add the ginger and garlic, and stir fry them until the ginger is light brown — about two minutes. Add the beef along with its marinade, and stir fry it until no traces of pink remain — one to two minutes. Spoon the beef mixture onto the center of the vegetables and keep the platter warm.

Pour the stock into the skillet or wok, and bring it to a boil. While the stock is heating, mix the remaining cornstarch with 2 tablespoons of water in a small bowl. Stir into the stock the cornstarch mixture, chili sauce or red-pepper-flake mixture, the remaining tablespoon of sugar, the lemon juice, and the hoisin sauce or soy sauce. Reduce the heat and simmer the mixture until it thickens — about one minute. Pour the sauce over the beef and serve it immediately.

Orange-Fried Beef

Serves 6
Working (and total) time: about 45 minutes

Calories **270**
Protein **24g.**
Cholesterol **63mg.**
Total fat **10g.**
Saturated fat **3g.**
Sodium **140mg.**

1½ lb. boneless sirloin steak, trimmed of fat and sliced into very thin strips
2 oranges
1 tbsp. grated lemon zest
3 tbsp. cornstarch
2 tbsp. sugar
2 tbsp. safflower oil
2 tsp. julienned fresh ginger
¼ tsp. salt
⅛ tsp. cayenne pepper
¼ cup rice vinegar or distilled white vinegar
1 lb. snow peas, stems and strings removed

Carefully pare the zest from the oranges with a sharp knife, leaving the white pith behind. Slice the zest into fine julienne — you should have about ½ cup — and reserve it.

Squeeze the juice from the oranges and pour it into a small saucepan. Boil the juice over medium heat until only 3 tablespoons remain and set it aside.

Put the beef into a large bowl and sprinkle it with the lemon zest, cornstarch and sugar. Mix well to coat the beef and set the beef aside.

Heat 1 tablespoon of the safflower oil in a large, nonstick skillet or a well-seasoned wok over high heat. Add the orange zest and the ginger to the skillet or wok, and cook them, stirring constantly, for one minute. Remove the zest and ginger with a slotted spoon, and set the mixture aside.

Add one third of the beef to the hot skillet or wok, distributing it in a single layer. Brown the beef well — it should take three to four minutes to cook — stirring it frequently. With a slotted spoon, remove the cooked beef. Add ½ tablespoon of the oil to the skillet or wok and repeat the process with another third of the beef. Remove the second batch. Heat the remaining ½ tablespoon of oil and cook the rest of the meat.

Once the third batch is well browned, return the already-cooked beef and the zest-and-ginger mixture to the skillet or wok. Sprinkle the meat with the salt and the cayenne pepper, then pour in the vinegar and the reduced orange juice. Cook the meat rapidly, stirring often, until all the liquid has evaporated — approximately two minutes.

While the beef is cooking, pour enough water into a saucepan to cover the bottom by 1 inch. Set a vegetable steamer in the water, bring the water to a boil, and add the snow peas. Cover the pan tightly and steam the peas for two minutes.

Transfer the peas to a warmed serving platter and mound the beef on top. Serve immediately.

SUGGESTED ACCOMPANIMENT: *steamed rice.*

Stir-Fried Beef with Pine Nuts on Nappa Cabbage

Serves 4
Working (and total) time: about 20 minutes

Calories **225**
Protein **19g.**
Cholesterol **54mg.**
Total fat **13g.**
Saturated fat **3g.**
Sodium **165mg.**

1 lb. beef tenderloin, trimmed of fat and cut into thin strips
4 tsp. cornstarch
1 tsp. freshly ground black pepper
1 tsp. oyster sauce
1 tsp. low-sodium soy sauce
1 tbsp. dry sherry
½ tsp. sugar
1½ tbsp. safflower oil
⅓ cup finely chopped onion
½ green pepper, seeded, deribbed and finely chopped
1 celery stalk, finely chopped
1 scallion, trimmed and thinly sliced
8 Nappa cabbage leaves or iceberg lettuce leaves, washed and dried
2 tbsp. pine nuts

Put the beef strips into a bowl and sprinkle them with 2 teaspoons of the cornstarch and the pepper. Toss the strips to coat them and let them stand at room tem-perature while you prepare the remaining ingredients.

In a small bowl, combine the remaining 2 teaspoons of cornstarch, the oyster sauce, soy sauce, sherry and sugar. Set the bowl aside.

Heat the oil in a large, nonstick skillet or a well-seasoned wok over high heat. When the oil is hot, add the beef strips and stir fry them until the meat lightens in color but is still slightly pink — one to two minutes. Use a slotted spoon to transfer the meat to a plate; set the plate aside.

Return the skillet or wok to high heat. Add the on-ion, green pepper and celery and stir fry them for 30 seconds. Return the meat to the pan, then cook the mixture, stirring continuously, until it is hot — 10 to 15 seconds. Pour the oyster-sauce mixture over the ingre-dients in the skillet or wok. Stir fry the meat and vege-tables until the sauce thickens and coats them — 30 seconds to one minute. Remove the pan from the heat.

Toss the scallion with the beef and vegetables. Set two cabbage or lettuce leaves on each plate; divide the mixture among the leaves. Sprinkle the pine nuts over the beef and vegetables and serve immediately.

SUGGESTED ACCOMPANIMENT: *rice noodle and shredded car-rot salad.*
EDITOR'S NOTE: *If oyster sauce is not available, you may substi-tute an additional teaspoon of low-sodium soy sauce.*

Top Round
Sautéed with Broccoli

Serves 6
Working (and total) time: about 40 minutes

Calories **250**
Protein **27g.**
Cholesterol **60mg.**
Total fat **11g.**
Saturated fat **3g.**
Sodium **355mg.**

1½ lb. top round steak, trimmed of fat and cut into very thin strips about 1½ inches long
1½ tsp. chili paste, or ½ tsp. hot red-pepper flakes
4 garlic cloves, very finely chopped
1½ cups unsalted brown stock or unsalted chicken stock (recipes, page 137)
1 tbsp. cornstarch
1 lb. broccoli, the stalks peeled and cut into thin strips about 1½ inches long, the tops cut into small florets
1¼ lb. cauliflower (about ½ large head), cut into small florets
2 tbsp. safflower oil
½ tsp. salt
2 lemons, peeled and cut into ½-inch pieces

Put the steak strips into a bowl with the chili paste or pepper flakes and the garlic, and let them marinate while you prepare the other ingredients.

Pour the stock into a small saucepan and boil it until about ⅔ cup remains. In a small bowl, mix 2 table-spoons of the reduced stock with the cornstarch.

Blanch the broccoli and cauliflower together in 3 quarts of boiling water for one minute. Drain the vege-tables, refresh them under cold running water, and drain them once more.

Heat 1 tablespoon of the safflower oil in a large, nonstick skillet or a well-seasoned wok over high heat. When the oil is hot, add the vegetables, then sprinkle them with the salt, and sauté the mixture for two min-utes. With a slotted spoon, transfer the vegetables to a serving bowl.

Pour the remaining tablespoon of oil into the skillet or wok. Add the marinated steak strips and sauté them until they are lightly browned — about one minute.

Return the vegetables to the skillet or wok. Pour in the stock and the cornstarch mixture, then add half the lemon pieces. Cook the mixture, stirring, for a minute and a half, then use a slotted spoon to transfer it to a serving dish. Boil the sauce remaining in the pan until it is reduced to about ½ cup, and pour it over the meat and vegetables. Scatter the remaining lemon pieces over the top and serve immediately.

Sautéed Beef Tossed with Red Cabbage and Apples

Serves 8
Working time: about 30 minutes
Total time: about 45 minutes

Calories **220**
Protein **19g.**
Cholesterol **50mg.**
Total fat **7g.**
Saturated fat **2g.**
Sodium **145mg.**

1¾ lb. sirloin steak, trimmed of fat and cut into thin strips about 1½ inches long
¼ cup chopped shallots
¼ tsp. salt
1 cup unsalted brown stock or unsalted chicken stock (recipes, page 137)
2 cups red wine
2 tsp. caraway seeds
1 small red cabbage (about 2½ lb.), cored, quartered and sliced
2 tart green apples, cored, quartered and cut into strips 2 inches long and ¼ inch wide
1 tbsp. honey
¼ cup fresh lemon juice
1 tsp. freshly ground black pepper
1½ tbsp. safflower oil
2 scallions, trimmed and sliced

Combine the shallots, salt, stock, wine and 1 teaspoon of the caraway seeds in a nonreactive saucepan over medium heat. Simmer the liquid until it is reduced to ½ cup — about 40 minutes.

Meanwhile, place the cabbage in a large bowl with the apples and the remaining teaspoon of caraway seeds. Mix the honey and lemon juice, and pour it over the cabbage mixture. Toss the mixture well and set it aside.

Place the meat in a bowl and sprinkle it with the pepper. Pour the reduced liquid over the meat and stir the mixture well.

Heat 1 tablespoon of the oil in a large, heavy-bottomed skillet set over high heat. Add the beef and scallions and sauté them, stirring, until the meat is browned — about one and a half minutes. Transfer the mixture to a bowl.

Heat the remaining ½ tablespoon of oil in the skillet over medium-high heat. Add the cabbage-and-apple mixture and cook it, stirring frequently, until the cabbage has wilted slightly — three to four minutes. Return the beef to the skillet, toss the mixture well, and serve it at once.

SUGGESTED ACCOMPANIMENT: *broad egg noodles.*

Stir-Fried Ginger Beef with Watercress

Serves 4
Working time: about 20 minutes
Total time: about 1 hour and 10 minutes

Calories **195**
Protein **21g.**
Cholesterol **54mg.**
Total fat **7g.**
Saturated fat **2g.**
Sodium **440mg.**

1 lb. top round steak, trimmed of fat and sliced into thin strips 3 inches long
½ tbsp. peanut oil
1 bunch watercress, trimmed, washed and dried
Ginger marinade
one 2-inch piece fresh ginger, peeled and finely chopped
1 tbsp. chili paste, or 1 tsp. hot red-pepper flakes
¼ cup dry sherry
¼ cup unsalted chicken stock (recipe, page 137)
cornstarch
1 tsp. sugar
Cucumber salad
2 cucumbers, seeded and cut into thick strips
¼ tsp. salt
¼ cup rice vinegar or distilled white vinegar
1 tsp. dark sesame oil

Combine all of the marinade ingredients in a bowl. Add the beef and toss it well; cover the bowl and marinate the meat for one hour at room temperature.

Combine the cucumbers, salt, vinegar and sesame oil in a bowl. Refrigerate the salad.

When the marinating time is up, drain the beef, reserving the marinade. Heat the oil in a large, nonstick skillet or a well-seasoned wok over high heat. Add the beef and stir fry it until it is well browned — about two minutes. Add the reserved marinade; stir constantly until the sauce thickens — about one minute. Add the watercress and toss the mixture quickly. Serve the stir-fried beef and watercress immediately, accompanied by the chilled cucumber salad.

SUGGESTED ACCOMPANIMENT: *rice with sweet red peppers.*

Beef Braised in Beer

Serves 8
Working time: about 30 minutes
Total time: about 3 hours

Calories **290**	*one 2½-lb. arm pot roast, trimmed of fat*
Protein **31g.**	*½ tsp. safflower oil*
Cholesterol **85mg.**	*8 large onions (about 4 lb.), sliced*
Total fat **8g.**	*2 cups unsalted brown stock or unsalted chicken stock*
Saturated fat **3g.**	*(recipes, page 137)*
Sodium **240mg.**	*2 tbsp. flour*
	12 oz. dark beer
	4 garlic cloves, chopped
	2 tbsp. julienned fresh ginger
	1 bay leaf
	4 fresh thyme sprigs, or 1 tsp. dried thyme leaves
	1 strip of lemon zest
	2 tbsp. dark molasses
	½ tsp. salt
	freshly ground black pepper

Preheat the oven to 325° F. Heat the oil in a large, nonstick skillet over high heat. Add the pot roast and sear it until it is well browned on both sides — about five minutes in all. Transfer the roast to an ovenproof casserole or Dutch oven.

Reduce the heat under the skillet to medium. Add the onions to the skillet and cook them, stirring frequently, until they begin to soften — about 10 minutes. Deglaze the pan with two tablespoons of the stock. Continue cooking the onions, adding another two tablespoons of stock whenever the liquid in the skillet has evaporated, until the onions are very soft and their juices have caramelized — 15 to 20 minutes more. Sprinkle the flour over the onions; cook the mixture, stirring constantly, for one minute.

Pour 1 cup of the remaining stock into the skillet and stir well to incorporate the flour. Increase the heat to medium high and boil the mixture until it is quite thick — three to four minutes. Pour in the rest of the stock and the beer. Bring the liquid to a simmer, then transfer the contents of the skillet to the casserole or Dutch oven. Add the garlic, ginger, bay leaf, thyme, lemon zest, molasses, salt and some pepper to the casserole. Cover the pan and braise the roast in the oven until it is very tender — about two hours.

Transfer the roast to a cutting board, slice it, and arrange the slices on a serving platter. Remove the bay leaf, the thyme sprigs if you used them, and the lemon zest from the sauce, and pour it over the meat.

SUGGESTED ACCOMPANIMENTS: *noodles tossed with fresh parsley; steamed parsnips.*

Lemon-Cardamom Braised Beef

Serves 8
Working time: about 1 hour
Total time: about 3 hours

Calories **240**
Protein **29g.**
Cholesterol **78mg.**
Total fat **8g.**
Saturated fat **3g.**
Sodium **290mg.**

one 3-lb. tip roast, trimmed of fat
2 tsp. safflower oil
2 onions, cut into eighths
2 celery stalks, coarsely chopped
2 garlic cloves, chopped
3 cups unsalted brown stock or unsalted chicken stock, (recipes, page 137)
½ cup dry white wine
zest of 1 lemon, cut into strips
½ tsp. ground cardamom or ground ginger
½ tsp. salt
2½ tbsp. fresh lemon juice
1 tbsp. Dijon mustard
freshly ground black pepper
1 lb. carrots
1 lb. zucchini, halved lengthwise, the halves sliced on the diagonal into ½-inch-wide pieces

Heat the oil in a Dutch oven or a large, deep skillet over high heat. Sear the beef until it is browned on all sides — 10 to 15 minutes. Tuck the onions, celery and garlic around the beef, and add the stock, wine, lemon zest, ¼ teaspoon of the cardamom or ginger, and ¼ teaspoon of the salt. Bring the liquid to a boil, then lower the heat to maintain a slow simmer. Cover the skillet, leaving the lid slightly ajar, and braise the beef for one hour. Turn the beef over and continue cooking it until it is tender — one hour and 30 minutes to two hours. Transfer the beef to a cutting board and cover it loosely with aluminum foil.

Strain the cooking liquid through a fine sieve into a saucepan. Whisk in 1½ tablespoons of the lemon juice, the mustard, a generous grinding of pepper, the remaining ¼ teaspoon of cardamom or ginger, and the remaining ¼ teaspoon of salt. Simmer the sauce over medium heat until it is reduced to 1¼ cups.

While the sauce is reducing, peel the carrots and cut them with a roll cut. Using a chef's knife, slice off the tip of a carrot on the diagonal. Roll the carrot a half turn and slice off another piece — it will have nonparallel ends. Continue rolling and slicing until you reach the stem end. Repeat the procedure to prepare the remaining carrots.

Pour enough water into a saucepan to fill it 1 inch deep. Set a vegetable steamer in the pan and bring the water to a boil. Add the carrots and cover the pan ▶

tightly. Steam the carrots until they begin to soften — five to seven minutes. Transfer them to a large skillet over medium-high heat. Add the zucchini, the remaining 1 tablespoon of lemon juice, ½ cup of the sauce and a liberal grinding of pepper. Cook the vegetables, stirring frequently, until almost all of the liquid has evaporated and the vegetables are glazed —

seven to 10 minutes.

Cut the beef into thin slices and arrange them on a warmed serving platter along with the vegetables. Briefly reheat the remaining sauce and pour it over the beef. Serve immediately.

SUGGESTED ACCOMPANIMENT: *whole-grain muffins.*

Beef Braised with Fennel

Serves 4
Working time: about 15 minutes
Total time: about 1 hour and 15 minutes

Calories **245**
Protein **27g.**
Cholesterol **76mg.**
Total fat **10g.**
Saturated fat **3g.**
Sodium **250mg.**

one 1¼-lb. boneless sirloin steak, trimmed of fat and cut into 4 pieces
¼ tsp. salt
freshly ground black pepper
1 tbsp. safflower oil
1 large fennel bulb, thinly sliced
1 cup unsalted brown stock or unsalted chicken stock (recipes, page 137)
¼ cup dry white wine
1 large carrot, peeled and grated
1 tbsp. cornstarch, mixed with 2 tablespoons of water

With a meat mallet or the flat of a heavy knife, pound the steak pieces to a thickness of ½ inch. Season the

meat with the salt and some pepper. Heat 1 teaspoon of the oil in a large, nonstick skillet over medium-high heat and sear the meat on both sides. Transfer the meat to a plate and set it aside.

Heat the remaining 2 teaspoons of oil in the skillet and add the fennel. Cook the fennel, stirring occasionally, until it begins to brown — 10 to 12 minutes. Return the meat to the skillet. Pour in the stock and white wine and, if necessary, enough water to raise the liquid level two thirds up the side of the meat. Bring the liquid to a simmer, cover the skillet, and braise the meat for 25 minutes. Turn the pieces and continue cooking them for 20 minutes.

Stir the carrot into the skillet and cook it for 10 minutes. Whisk the cornstarch mixture into the simmering liquid; stir constantly until the sauce thickens slightly. Serve the beef and fennel immediately.

SUGGESTED ACCOMPANIMENT: *lettuce and tomato salad.*

Roulades in Tomato Sauce

Serves 8
Working time: about 1 hour and 30 minutes
Total time: about 4 hours

Calories **235**	one 2-lb. top round roast, trimmed of fat and cut on the diagonal into 16 scallopini
Protein **25g.**	
Cholesterol **57mg.**	1 tsp. safflower oil
Total fat **8g.**	3 onions, finely chopped
Saturated fat **3g.**	4 garlic cloves, finely chopped
Sodium **165mg.**	2 carrots, finely chopped
	56 oz. canned unsalted whole tomatoes, with their juice
	2 bay leaves
	3 tbsp. chopped parsley
	2 tbsp. chopped fresh oregano, or 2 tsp. dried oregano
	½ cup dry bread crumbs
	¼ cup freshly grated Parmesan cheese
	2 tbsp. finely chopped prosciutto or boiled ham
	¼ cup dry white wine

Mix the oil, onions, garlic and carrots in a large, heavy-bottomed saucepan. Cover the pan and cook the mix-ture over low heat until the onions are translucent — about 15 minutes.

Purée the tomatoes in a food processor or a blender. Add the purée and bay leaves to the onion-and-carrot mixture. Increase the heat to medium and simmer the vegetables, uncovered, until they become a thick sauce — about two hours.

While the sauce is simmering, make the roulades. In a bowl, combine the parsley, oregano, bread crumbs, cheese, prosciutto or ham, and the wine. Spread the scallopini flat on the work surface and spread some of the stuffing mixture on each one. Roll up each slice and tie it with two short pieces of string to secure it.

Add the roulades to the thickened sauce and sim-mer them until the meat is tender — about one hour. Lift the roulades from the sauce and remove the string. Spoon the sauce over the roulades and serve them immediately.

SUGGESTED ACCOMPANIMENT: *fettuccine.*

Cabbage Rolls with Beef and Sage

Serves 6
Working time: about 30 minutes
Total time: about 2 hours

Calories **305**
Protein **27g.**
Cholesterol **60mg.**
Total fat **9g.**
Saturated fat **3g.**
Sodium **250mg.**

one 1½-lb. top round steak, trimmed of fat and cut on the diagonal into 12 thin slices
1 large green cabbage (about 4 lb.)
1 tbsp. safflower oil
2 cups chopped onion
1 tbsp. chopped fresh sage, or 1 tsp. dried sage
4 garlic cloves, finely chopped
3 slices white bread, crumbled
½ cup stemmed parsley sprigs
28 oz. canned unsalted whole tomatoes, crushed in their juice
3 carrots, thinly sliced
3 tbsp. cider vinegar
1½ tbsp. sugar
¼ tsp. salt
freshly ground black pepper

Carefully remove 12 large outer leaves from the cabbage. Cut a small V-shaped wedge from each leaf to remove the tough core. Cook the leaves in a large pot of boiling water until they are translucent and limp — about 10 minutes. Drain the leaves in a colander.

Finely slice enough of the remaining cabbage to yield 5 cups. Save the rest for future use.

To prepare the filling, heat the oil in a large heavy-bottomed or nonstick skillet over medium heat. Add the sliced cabbage, 1½ cups of the onion, 2 teaspoons of the fresh sage or ½ teaspoon of the dried sage, and half of the garlic. Cook the mixture, stirring occasionally, until the onion is translucent and the cabbage is soft — about 10 minutes. Transfer the mixture to a bowl, add the bread and parsley, and toss well. Set the filling aside.

Meanwhile, put the tomatoes and their juice, the remaining garlic, the carrots and ¾ cup of water into a very large skillet. Cook the mixture, stirring occasionally, over low heat for 15 minutes. Add the remaining ½ cup of onion, the vinegar, the sugar, the remaining sage, the salt and some pepper. Allow the sauce to simmer slowly while you prepare the rolls.

With a meat mallet or the flat of a heavy knife, pound the beef slices between two pieces of heavy-duty plastic wrap to a thickness of ⅛ inch. Sprinkle the slices with some pepper.

Set a cabbage leaf on a work surface with the stem end toward you. Lay a beef slice atop the leaf, then mound 2 heaping tablespoons of the filling on the beef. Roll up the leaf starting at the stem end; fold in the sides over the filling as you go. Repeat the process with the remaining leaves, meat and filling.

Place the cabbage rolls, seam sides down, in the simmering sauce. Cook the rolls, with the skillet lid slightly ajar, over low to medium-low heat for one hour and 15 minutes. Carefully transfer the rolls to a platter. Spoon the sauce over them and serve immediately.

SUGGESTED ACCOMPANIMENT: *barley-mushroom pilaf.*

Braised Cinnamon Beef Roll

Serves 4
Working time: about 25 minutes
Total time: about 2 hours

Calories **250**
Protein **28g.**
Cholesterol **72mg.**
Total fat **11g.**
Saturated fat **3g.**
Sodium **215mg.**

one 1¼-lb. top round, rump or tip roast, trimmed of fat and cut into 4 slices
1 tbsp. ground cinnamon
¼ tsp. salt
freshly ground black pepper
1 tbsp. safflower oil
1 large onion, thinly sliced
1 garlic clove, finely chopped
2 cinnamon sticks
½ cup dry white wine
1 cup unsalted brown stock or unsalted chicken stock (recipes, page 137)
1 tbsp. cornstarch, mixed with 1 tbsp. of the stock

Place the beef slices between two sheets of plastic wrap or wax paper and pound them with a meat mallet or the flat of a heavy knife to a thickness of ⅛ inch. Sprinkle the meat with the ground cinnamon, the salt and some pepper. Overlap the edges of two slices, spiced side up; cover the seam thus formed with plastic wrap or wax paper and lightly pound the overlapping edges to join the slices. Join the remaining two slices together by the same procedure.

Place one of the joined pieces on top of the other, again spiced side up, then roll them up tightly, starting with one of the longer edges. To hold the roll together, tie it with butcher's twine *(technique, page 25)*.

Heat 1 teaspoon of the oil in a heavy-bottomed skillet over medium-high heat and sear the beef on all sides. Remove the meat; add the remaining 2 teaspoonfuls of oil and the onion to the skillet, and cook the onion over medium heat, stirring occasionally, until it is translucent — four to five minutes. Stir in the garlic, cinnamon sticks, wine and stock. Return the beef to the skillet and, if necessary, pour in enough water to half submerge the roll. Bring the liquid to a simmer,

cover the skillet tightly, and continue simmering the roll until the meat feels tender when pierced with the tip of a sharp knife — one hour and 15 minutes to one hour and 30 minutes.

When the beef roll is cooked, transfer it to a plate. Increase the heat to medium high and bring the liquid in the skillet to a boil. Remove the cinnamon sticks and discard them. Whisk the cornstarch paste into the liquid, whisking continuously until the sauce thickens — about 30 seconds.

Remove the string, slice the meat thinly, and place the slices on a warm serving platter. Top them with some of the sauce, pouring the rest around the beef. Serve immediately.

SUGGESTED ACCOMPANIMENT: *brown rice tossed with scallions and raisins.*

two to three hours. Remove the pot roast from the casserole without discarding the cooking liquid; keep the roast warm.

Add the carrots, the celeriac or celery, the onions, and the parsnips or turnips to the cooking liquid. Simmer the vegetables until they are tender — approximately 20 minutes.

Cut the roast into slices and arrange them on a serving platter. Surround the meat with the vegetables. Spoon some of the cooking liquid over the meat and pour the rest into a sauce bowl to be passed separately.

Pot Roast with Parsnips

Serves 10
Working time: about 30 minutes
Total time: about 2 hours and 30 minutes

Calories **290**
Protein **33g.**
Cholesterol **93mg.**
Total fat **10g.**
Saturated fat **3g.**
Sodium **215mg.**

one 3½-lb. arm pot roast, trimmed of fat
1 tbsp. safflower oil
1 cup unsalted brown stock or unsalted chicken stock (recipes, page 137)
14 oz. canned unsalted tomatoes, puréed and strained
2 garlic cloves, finely chopped
½ tsp. salt
10 crushed black peppercorns
1 bay leaf
1 tbsp. chopped fresh thyme; or 1 tsp. dried thyme leaves
3 carrots, peeled and cut diagonally into ½-inch-thick ovals
¾ lb. celeriac, peeled and cut into ½-inch cubes, or 3 celery stalks, cut into ½-inch pieces
5 small onions, peeled and halved crosswise
1 lb. parsnips, peeled and cut into ½-inch pieces, or 1 lb. turnips, peeled and cut into ½-inch pieces

Heat the oil in a large, heavy-bottomed casserole over medium-high heat. Add the roast and brown it on both sides — one to two minutes per side — then pour in the stock and enough water to cover the meat. Add tomato purée, the garlic, salt, peppercorns, bay leaf and thyme, and bring the liquid to a boil. Reduce the heat to low, cover the casserole, and simmer the beef until it feels very tender when pierced with a fork —

Braised Steak with Onions

Serves 6
Working time: about 1 hour
Total time: about 2 hours and 30 minutes

Calories **175**
Protein **22g.**
Cholesterol **49mg.**
Total fat **5g.**
Saturated fat **2g.**
Sodium **195mg.**

one 1¾-lb. eye round roast, trimmed of fat and cut into 6 steaks
2 tsp. safflower oil
2 large onions, thinly sliced
2 cups red wine
2 carrots, cut into bâtonnets
1 celery stalk, chopped
¼ tsp. salt
freshly ground black pepper
2 cups unsalted brown stock or unsalted chicken stock (recipes, page 137)

Preheat the oven to 325° F.

Heat the oil in a large, ovenproof skillet over medium heat. Add the onions and cook them, stirring frequently, until they are translucent and their juices have caramelized — five to 10 minutes. Pour ½ cup of the wine into the skillet, increase the heat and boil the wine until nearly all the liquid has evaporated. Pour in another ½ cup and reduce this also. Boil away the remaining wine in two batches, stirring constantly as the last ½ cup begins to evaporate.

Add the carrots, celery, salt, some pepper and the stock to the skillet. Lay the steaks on top of the vegetables; cover the skillet and transfer it to the oven. Braise the steaks until they are tender — one and a half to two hours. Serve the steaks topped with the vegetables and braising juices.

SUGGESTED ACCOMPANIMENT: *potatoes and rutabagas mashed together and sprinkled with chopped parsley.*

Saffron-Rice Roulades with Black Beans

Serves 4
Working time: about 40 minutes
Total time: about 2 hours and 30 minutes
(includes soaking)

Calories **435**
Protein **38g.**
Cholesterol **73mg.**
Total fat **10g.**
Saturated fat **3g.**
Sodium **265mg.**

one 1¼-lb. top round steak (about ½ inch thick), trimmed of fat
¾ cup black beans, picked over
3 garlic cloves, finely chopped
10 drops hot red-pepper sauce
1 bay leaf
½ cup rice
1 scallion, finely chopped
8 saffron threads, or ½ tsp. annatto
¼ tsp. salt
freshly ground black pepper
1 green pepper, seeded, deribbed and coarsely chopped
2 tbsp. finely chopped pimento
1 tsp. safflower oil
2½ cups unsalted brown stock or unsalted chicken stock (recipes, page 137)
¼ cup red wine vinegar

Rinse the beans, then put them into a large, heavy-bottomed pot, and pour in enough water to cover them by about 3 inches. Discard any beans that float to the surface. Cover the pot, leaving the lid ajar, and slowly bring the liquid to a boil over medium-low heat. Boil the beans for two minutes, then turn off the heat, and soak the beans, covered, for at least one hour. (Alternatively, soak the beans overnight in cold water.)

Drain the beans in a colander and return them to the pot. Pour in 1¼ cups of water, then add about two thirds of the garlic, the hot red-pepper sauce and the bay leaf. Slowly bring the liquid to a boil over medium-low heat. Reduce the heat to maintain a simmer and cover the pot. Cook the beans, stirring occasionally and skimming any foam from the surface, until they are tender — about one hour and 15 minutes.

While the beans are simmering, cook the rice. Combine the rice, scallion, saffron threads or annatto and 1 cup of water in a small saucepan. Bring the liquid to a simmer over medium-low heat, cover the pan, and cook the rice until it is tender — about 20 minutes.

Cut the steak horizontally into two ¼-inch-thick slices. (Alternatively, have the butcher do this for you.) Place one of the beef slices between two sheets of plastic wrap or wax paper, and pound it with a meat mallet or the flat of a heavy knife to a thickness of ⅛ inch. Pound the other slice in the same manner.

Season the beef with ⅛ teaspoon of the salt and some pepper. Spread the rice mixture on the slices of

beef, and scatter the green pepper and pimento over it. Roll up the slices and tie them with butcher's twine.

Heat the oil in a nonstick skillet over medium-high heat. Sear the roulades on all sides in the oil. Add the remaining garlic and cook it, stirring continuously, for 30 seconds. Stir in the stock, vinegar and the remaining ⅛ teaspoon of salt, and bring the liquid to a simmer. Cover the pot and simmer the beef until it is tender — 45 minutes to one hour.

Remove the cooked meat from the skillet. Drain the beans and stir them into the braising liquid.

Remove the string from the roulades and slice them into 1-inch-thick rounds. Arrange the rounds on a platter and heap the beans in the middle; pour the braising liquid over them.

SUGGESTED ACCOMPANIMENT: *tomato and basil salad.*

Beef Paprika

Serves 4
Working time: about 20 minutes
Total time: about 2 hours

Calories **215**
Protein **28g.**
Cholesterol **76mg.**
Total fat **11g.**
Saturated fat **3g.**
Sodium **235mg.**

one 1¼-lb. boneless sirloin steak, trimmed of fat and cut into 4 pieces
¼ tsp. salt
freshly ground black pepper
2½ tbsp. paprika, preferably Hungarian
2 tbsp. flour
1 tbsp. safflower oil
1 onion, cut into 1-inch cubes
1 green pepper, seeded, deribbed and cut into 1-inch squares
1 garlic clove, finely chopped
1½ cups unsalted brown stock or unsalted chicken stock (recipes, page 137)
¼ lb. mushrooms, wiped clean, the large ones cut in half

Season the pieces of beef with the salt and some pepper. Combine 2 tablespoons of the paprika and the flour on a plate. Dredge the pieces in this mixture, coating each one evenly. Reserve the remaining flour-paprika mixture.

Heat 1 teaspoon of the oil in a nonstick skillet over medium-high heat. Sear the meat in the skillet and set it aside. Wipe the pan clean with a paper towel; heat the remaining 2 teaspoons of oil in it. Add the onion, green pepper and garlic, and sauté them, stirring occasionally, until the onions are translucent — about five minutes. Add the remaining flour-paprika mixture, then whisk in the stock.

Add the meat and bring the stock to a simmer. Cover the pan and simmer the beef and vegetables for one hour and 15 minutes. Stir in the mushrooms and the remaining ½ tablespoon of paprika; cook the mixture,

covered, for 15 minutes longer.

Serve the beef surrounded by the vegetables and covered with the sauce.

SUGGESTED ACCOMPANIMENTS: *egg noodles; broccoli.*

Steak Braised in
Spicy Vinegar Sauce

Serves 4
Working time: about 15 minutes
Total time: about 4 hours and 15 minutes
(includes marinating)

Calories **235**
Protein **28g.**
Cholesterol **78mg.**
Total fat **11g.**
Saturated fat **3g.**
Sodium **245mg.**

one 1¼-lb. boneless sirloin steak, trimmed of fat and cut into 4 pieces
1 garlic clove, finely chopped
1 tbsp. chopped fresh oregano, or 1 tsp. dried oregano
hot red-pepper flakes
¼ cup balsamic vinegar, or 3 tbsp. red wine vinegar mixed with 1 tsp. honey
1 tbsp. safflower oil
¼ tsp. salt
freshly ground black pepper
14 oz. canned unsalted whole tomatoes, with their juice
2 tbsp. freshly grated Parmesan cheese
parsley sprigs

Put the pieces of meat into a shallow, nonreactive dish and add the garlic, oregano, a pinch of red pepper flakes and the vinegar. Let the meat marinate for three hours in the refrigerator. Drain the meat and pat the pieces dry, reserving the marinade.

Heat the oil in a large, heavy-bottomed casserole over medium-high heat. Sear the meat on both sides, then season it with the salt and some black pepper. Purée the tomatoes in a food processor or a blender and add them and the reserved marinade to the skillet. Cover it and simmer the meat in the sauce for 30 minutes. Turn the meat, replace the cover, and continue braising the pieces until they are tender — approximately 30 to 45 minutes.

Transfer the beef to a heated platter and spoon the sauce over it. Serve the dish topped with the grated cheese and garnished with parsley sprigs.

SUGGESTED ACCOMPANIMENTS: *pasta tossed with some of the spicy vinegar sauce; steamed zucchini.*

Beef Curry

Serves 8
Working time: about 25 minutes
Total time: about 2 hours

Calories **265**
Protein **22g.**
Cholesterol **54mg.**
Total fat **8g.**
Saturated fat **2g.**
Sodium **140mg.**

2 lb. top round, trimmed of fat and cut into ½-inch pieces
2 cups unsalted brown stock or unsalted chicken stock (recipes, page 137)
1 cup dry white wine
1 onion, chopped
1 carrot, thinly sliced on the diagonal
¾ cup chopped, pitted prunes
1 pear, peeled, quartered, cored and thinly sliced
1 tbsp. honey
2 tsp. curry powder
¼ tsp. salt
1 tbsp. safflower oil
2 plantains or bananas, cut into ¼-inch rounds
1½ tbsp. fresh lemon juice

Combine the stock, wine and 1½ cups of water in a large, heavy-bottomed, nonreactive pot and bring the liquid to a boil. Add the beef and reduce the heat to medium low; cook the meat with the lid slightly ajar for 30 minutes, skimming the surface of the liquid from time to time.

Add the onion, carrot, prunes, pear, honey, curry powder and salt, and continue cooking slowly until the meat is very tender and the sauce has thickened — about one hour.

Ten minutes before serving, heat the oil in a large, heavy-bottomed or nonstick skillet over medium-high heat. Add the plantains or bananas and cook them, turning them occasionally, until they begin to brown. Sprinkle the fruit with the lemon juice; continue cooking the fruit until it has browned — about 10 minutes for plantains, five minutes for bananas.

To serve, mound the curry in the center of a warmed serving platter and surround it with the plantains or bananas. Serve at once.

SUGGESTED ACCOMPANIMENT: *brown rice tossed with peas and grated lemon zest.*

Chuckwagon Beef Stew with Corn-Flour Dumplings

Serves 4
Working time: about 15 minutes
Total time: about 1 hour

Calories **480**
Protein **29g.**
Cholesterol **59mg.**
Total fat **11g.**
Saturated fat **3g.**
Sodium **470mg.**

1 lb. beef round, trimmed of fat and cut into ½-inch cubes	
1 tsp. safflower oil	
2 garlic cloves, finely chopped	
1 onion, cut into ¾-inch cubes	
1 green pepper, seeded, deribbed and cut into ¾-inch squares	
½ cup rice	

⅛ tsp. cayenne pepper
¼ tsp. ground cumin
¼ tsp. salt
2 cups unsalted brown stock or unsalted chicken stock (recipes, page 137)
2 ears of corn, each cut into 4 pieces
1 large ripe tomato, peeled, seeded and coarsely chopped
Corn-flour dumplings
1 cup instant masa harina or stone-ground cornmeal
⅛ tsp. salt
1 ¼ tsp. baking powder
2 tsp. safflower oil
1 cup low-fat milk
2 tbsp. chopped fresh cilantro or parsley

Heat the oil in a large, nonstick skillet over medium-high heat. Sear the beef, tossing it continuously, until browned — about one minute. Add the garlic and cook for 45 seconds.

Reduce the heat to medium, stir in the onion, green pepper, rice, cayenne pepper, cumin, salt, stock and 2 cups of water, and bring the liquid to a simmer. Cover the skillet tightly and cook the mixture until the rice is tender — about 20 minutes.

To make the dumplings, combine the cornmeal, salt and baking powder in a bowl. Add the safflower oil and incorporate it, then pour in the milk, stirring with a wooden spoon to create a thick batter. Stir in the chopped cilantro or parsley and set the batter aside while the stew is cooking.

When the rice is done, add the corn and tomato and return the mixture to a simmer. Drop large spoonfuls of the batter into the stew; simmer the stew, covered, until the dumplings are cooked through — 12 to 15 minutes. Serve immediately.

SUGGESTED ACCOMPANIMENT: *cabbage salad.*

Spicy Beef Stew with Apricots and Olives

Serves 8
Working time: about 30 minutes
Total time: about 2 hours and 30 minutes

Calories **290**
Protein **29g.**
Cholesterol **72mg.**
Total fat **11g.**
Saturated fat **3g.**
Sodium **275mg.**

2½ lb. top round, trimmed of fat and cut into 1½-inch cubes
1 tbsp. safflower oil
3 onions, chopped
4 garlic cloves, finely chopped
14 oz. canned unsalted whole tomatoes, chopped, with their juice
2 cups unsalted brown stock or unsalted chicken stock (recipes, page 137)
½ cup red wine
1½ tsp. ground cumin
1½ tsp. ground coriander
⅛ tsp. cayenne pepper
¼ lb. dried apricots, halved
16 pitted green olives, rinsed and drained

Heat the oil in a large, heavy-bottomed skillet over medium heat. Add the onions, cook them, stirring often, until they are translucent — about five minutes. With a slotted spoon, transfer the onions to a heat-proof casserole.

Increase the heat to medium high. Add the beef cubes to the skillet and brown them on all sides — five to seven minutes.

Brown the beef in the skillet over medium-high heat. Transfer the beef to the casserole and add the garlic, the tomatoes and their juice, the stock, wine, cumin, coriander and cayenne pepper. Cover the casserole and reduce the heat to low; simmer the beef, stirring occasionally, for one and a half hours.

Stir the apricots and olives into the casserole, and continue cooking the stew until the meat is tender — about 30 minutes more. Transfer the stew to a bowl or a deep platter, and serve.

SUGGESTED ACCOMPANIMENT: *rice tossed with scallions, currants and sweet red pepper.*

Bollito Misto

THIS LIGHTER VERSION OF THE CLASSIC ITALIAN BOILED DINNER
CALLS FOR COOKING THE BEEF GENTLY FOR A LONG TIME. IF YOU
LIKE, THE DISH MAY BE PREPARED IN ADVANCE AND REHEATED.

Serves 16
Working time: about 1 hour and 15 minutes
Total time: about 6 hours

Calories **280**
Protein **33g.**
Cholesterol **92mg.**
Total fat **9g.**
Saturated fat **3g.**
Sodium **220mg.**

one 4-lb. arm pot roast, trimmed of fat
one 3-lb. chicken
16 carrots, cut into 2½-inch lengths
10 celery stalks, cut into 2½-inch lengths
2 onions, quartered
2 bay leaves
8 peppercorns
2 fresh thyme sprigs, or ½ tsp. dried thyme leaves
2 unpeeled garlic cloves
16 small white onions, peeled

Red sauce

28 oz. canned unsalted whole tomatoes, with their juice
1 onion, finely chopped
3 tbsp. cider vinegar
¼ cup dry bread crumbs
¼ tsp. hot red-pepper flakes

Green sauce

¾ cup dry bread crumbs
2 tsp. capers, rinsed
2 tbsp. chopped parsley
3 garlic cloves
2 anchovies, rinsed and patted dry

Put the pot roast, about one cup each of the carrots and celery, the quartered onions, bay leaves, peppercorns, thyme and garlic cloves into a large pot. Pour in enough water to cover them; bring the water to a simmer over medium-low heat. Cook the beef and vegetables for three hours.

Add the chicken to the pot and, if necessary, enough water to cover it. Continue to simmer the mixture until the chicken is tender and its juices run clear when a thigh is pierced with the tip of a sharp knife — about 45 minutes. Remove the beef and chicken from the pot and set them aside. Reserve the broth.

While the meats are cooking, make the accompanying sauces. For the red sauce, purée the tomatoes with their juice in a food processor or a blender. Strain the purée into a nonreactive saucepan, and add the onion, vinegar, bread crumbs and pepper flakes. Simmer the mixture, stirring occasionally, for 45 minutes. Pour the sauce into a bowl and refrigerate it.

For the green sauce, purée the bread crumbs, capers, parsley, garlic, anchovies and ¾ cup of the broth from the pot in a food processor or a blender. Pour the sauce into a small bowl and refrigerate it.

Skim the fat from the broth. Strain the broth through a sieve lined with cheesecloth into a bowl;

discard the solids. Rinse out the pot, then pour the broth back into it. Add the remaining carrots and celery, and the white onions. Simmer the vegetables until they are tender — 20 to 30 minutes.

Return the beef and chicken to the pot, cover the pot, and simmer them until they are heated through — about 15 minutes. Carve the beef and chicken, dis-carding the chicken skin. Arrange the pieces on a warm serving platter and moisten them with some of the broth. Save the rest of the broth for future use. Place the vegetables around the meat and serve immediately, with the sauces passed in separate bowls.

SUGGESTED ACCOMPANIMENT: *green salad.*

Japanese Simmered Beef

THIS DISH IS A MEAL IN ITSELF. TRADITIONALLY, THE INGREDIENTS ARE PREPARED AND SERVED AT THE TABLE.

Serves 6
Working time: about 25 minutes
Total time: about 40 minutes

Calories **230**
Protein **20g.**
Cholesterol **37mg.**
Total fat **7g.**
Saturated fat **2g.**
Sodium **350mg.**

1 lb. beef tenderloin, trimmed of fat and thinly sliced against the grain
¼ lb. Japanese udon noodles or vermicelli
1 large carrot, thinly sliced on the diagonal
2 oz. shiitake or other fresh mushrooms, wiped clean, the stems discarded and the caps thinly sliced (about 1 cup)
3 scallions, julienned
1 cup Nappa cabbage, cut into chiffonade
½ lb. tofu, cut into ¾-inch-wide strips
6 cups unsalted brown stock or unsalted chicken stock (recipes, page 137), or a combination of both
2 tbsp. low-sodium soy sauce
2 tbsp. rice vinegar
1 tsp. finely chopped fresh ginger
1 tsp. finely chopped garlic
¼ tsp. dark sesame oil

Precook the noodles or vermicelli in 2 quarts of boiling water. Begin testing for doneness after eight minutes and cook them until they are *al dente.* Drain the noodles in a colander and rinse them under running water to keep them from sticking together. Drain them again and set them aside in a bowl.

Arrange the tenderloin slices, the vegetables and the tofu on a large plate.

Combine the stock, soy sauce, vinegar, ginger and garlic in an electric skillet, a wok or a fondue pot. Bring the mixture to a simmer and cook it for five minutes, then add the sesame oil.

Begin the meal by cooking pieces of the beef in the simmering broth. After the meat has been eaten, cook the vegetables and tofu in the broth just until they are warmed through — three to four minutes. Finish the meal with the noodles or vermicelli, adding them to the broth and heating them. They may be eaten with the broth or served on their own.

Sirloin-Filled Pita Sandwiches

Serves 6
Working (and total) time: about 1 hour and 15 minutes

Calories **300**
Protein **22g.**
Cholesterol **38mg.**
Total fat **11g.**
Saturated fat **3g.**
Sodium **205mg.**

¾ lb. sirloin steak, trimmed of fat and thinly sliced
1 red onion, thickly sliced
6 whole-wheat pita breads
¼ lb. part-skim mozzarella, grated
3 garlic cloves, finely chopped
12 Kalamata olives or black olives, pitted and chopped
2 large ripe tomatoes, each cut into 6 slices
1 tbsp. safflower oil

Put the onion slices on the rack of a broiler pan and broil them until they are soft — about four minutes. Remove the onions from the rack and set them aside. Lay the slices of meat on the rack and broil them until they are browned — about two minutes.

Split a pita bread into two rounds. On the bottom half, layer one sixth of the onion, beef, cheese, garlic, olives and tomatoes. Set the top half in place. Repeat the process to make five more sandwiches.

Lightly brush the outside of the sandwiches with the oil. Toast the sandwiches in a waffle iron or in a skillet over medium heat until the bread is crisp and brown and the cheese has melted — about four minutes. Cut each sandwich in two before serving.

Mexican Meat Loaf

Serves 6
Working time: about 1 hour
Total time: about 2 hours and 45 minutes
(includes rising)

Calories **430**
Protein **28g.**
Cholesterol **57mg.**
Total fat **11g.**
Saturated fat **4g.**
Sodium **275mg.**

1 ¼ lb. beef round, trimmed of fat and ground (box, page 8)
2 ancho chili peppers, or 1 sweet red pepper, seeded, deribbed and finely chopped
1 tbsp. safflower oil
1 large onion, finely chopped
1 green pepper, seeded, deribbed and finely chopped
2 garlic cloves, finely chopped
⅛ tsp. salt
¼ tsp. ground cumin
cayenne pepper
freshly ground black pepper
1 cup fresh bread crumbs
2 oz. grated Cheddar cheese (about ½ cup)
2 tbsp. light brown sugar
1 tbsp. cornmeal
Spiced Dough
1 package active dry yeast
¼ tsp. sugar
2¾ cups bread flour
¼ tsp. salt
1 jalapeño pepper, seeded, deribbed and finely chopped (caution, page 23)
1 tsp. dried oregano

To make the dough, pour ¼ cup of lukewarm water into a bowl and sprinkle the yeast and sugar into it. After two minutes, stir the mixture until the yeast and sugar are dissolved.

Sift 2½ cups of the flour and the salt into a large bowl. Stir in the chopped jalapeño pepper and the oregano. Make a well in the center, pour the yeast mixture and ¾ cup of lukewarm water into it, and stir the ingredients together with a wooden spoon. Mix the dough by hand until it feels slightly sticky. If the mixture is too wet and clings to your hands, work in the remaining ¼ cup of flour, a tablespoon at a time, until the dough can be gathered into a ball. Place the dough on a floured surface and knead it until it has become smooth and elastic — about 10 minutes.

Put the dough into a lightly oiled bowl, turn the dough over once to coat it with the oil, and cover it with a damp cloth. Set the bowl in a warm, draft-free place until the dough has doubled in volume — approximately one hour and 30 minutes. Meanwhile, prepare the meat filling.

Remove and discard the stems and seeds from the ancho chilies if you are using them. Chop the chilies coarsely and soak them in 1 cup of boiling water for 10 minutes. Meanwhile, combine 2 teaspoons of the oil, the onion, the green pepper and the sweet red pepper, if you are using it, in a heavy-bottomed or nonstick skillet over medium heat. Cook the mixture, stirring occasionally, until the onion is lightly browned; add the garlic and cook for an additional minute. Transfer the onion mixture to a large bowl and set it aside.

Wipe out the skillet with a paper towel and pour in the remaining teaspoon of oil, tilting the skillet from side to side to distribute the oil. Add the beef and cook it over medium heat, crumbling it into small pieces with a wooden spoon. Cook the beef, stirring it constantly, until it loses its raw, red color. Sprinkle the beef with the salt, cumin, a pinch of cayenne pepper and some black pepper. Stir the mixture well and transfer it to the bowl containing the onion mixture; stir in the bread crumbs, cheese and brown sugar. If you are using the ancho chilies, purée them with ¾ cup of their soaking liquid in a food processor or a blender. Strain the purée through a sieve onto the onion-beef mixture, then stir it in. Set the mixture aside.

Preheat the oven to 425° F.

When the dough has doubled in volume, punch it down. Remove the dough from the bowl and roll it out on a lightly floured surface into a ¼-inch-thick rectangle measuring 10 inches by 16 inches. Transfer the dough to a baking sheet dusted with the cornmeal. Spoon the meat filling, slightly off center, in a straight line down the length of the rectangle, leaving a 2-inch border at either end. Brush the edges with a little water. Fold the wider side over the filling and securely seal the loaf by pressing its edges together. Tuck the ends under, and brush the surface of the dough with water to give it a hard crust. With a knife, lightly score the meat loaf's surface in a wide crisscross pattern. Bake the meat loaf for 10 minutes, then reduce the heat to 325° F., and bake the loaf for 30 minutes more. Transfer the meat loaf to a serving platter and allow it to rest for 10 to 15 minutes before slicing; then serve it.

SUGGESTED ACCOMPANIMENT: *mixed salad greens.*

Beet Hamburgers

Serves 8
Working time: about 20 minutes
Total time: about 2 hours

Calories **320**	2½ lb. beef round, trimmed of fat and ground, (box, page 8)
Protein **31g.**	
Cholesterol **71mg.**	2 lb. beets, washed, all but 1 inch of the stems cut off
Total fat **10g.**	1 small onion, peeled and grated
Saturated fat **3g.**	8 cornichons, chopped, or 2 small dill pickles, chopped
Sodium **310mg.**	¼ cup dry bread crumbs
	¼ cup distilled white vinegar
	freshly ground black pepper
	2 tsp. safflower oil
	½ cup unsalted brown stock or unsalted chicken stock (recipes, page 137)
	1 tsp. caraway seeds
	8 onion rolls, split

Preheat the oven to 400° F. Wrap all the beets together in a single package of aluminum foil and bake them until they are tender — approximately one hour. Unwrap the beets and let them cool. Peel and grate the beets. Put ½ cup of the beets into a bowl, and set the remainder aside.

Add the ground beef, onion, cornichons or pickles, bread crumbs, vinegar and some pepper to the bowl. Mix the ingredients thoroughly, then shape the mixture into eight patties.

Heat the oil in a large, nonstick skillet over medium-high heat. Add the patties to the skillet and brown them for about one minute per side. Add the reserved beets, the stock, caraway seeds and some pepper. Cover the skillet and reduce the heat to medium low. Simmer the mixture for 20 minutes.

Serve the hamburgers in the onion rolls, with the beets alongside.

SUGGESTED ACCOMPANIMENT: *cucumbers with dill.*

Beef and Potato Pie

Serves 4
Working time: about 1 hour
Total time: about 2 hours

Calories **485**	1¼ lb. beef round, trimmed of fat and ground (box, page 8)
Protein **32g.**	
Cholesterol **72mg.**	2 lb. potatoes, peeled and quartered
Total fat **12g.**	2 tbsp. skim milk
Saturated fat **3g.**	2 tbsp. chopped fresh parsley
Sodium **270mg.**	¼ tsp. salt
	4 tsp. safflower oil
	3 tbsp. flour
	2 cups unsalted brown stock or unsalted chicken stock (recipes, page 137)
	1 cup thinly sliced shallots or onions
	1 cup dried apples, chopped
	2 tbsp. cider vinegar
	1 tbsp. fresh thyme, or 1 tsp. dried thyme leaves
	freshly ground black pepper

Preheat the oven to 450° F.

Place the potatoes in a saucepan and add enough water to cover them. Bring the water to a boil, then reduce the heat, and simmer the potatoes until they are tender — 15 to 20 minutes. Drain the potatoes, spread them out on a baking sheet, and place them in the oven to dry. After five minutes, remove the pan from the oven and purée the potatoes by working them through a sieve or a food mill set over a bowl. Combine the potatoes with the milk, parsley and salt and set them aside.

Blend 2 teaspoons of the oil and the flour in a saucepan over low heat and cook the paste for one minute. Gradually whisk in the stock and simmer the mixture slowly over low heat until it thickens — about two min-

utes. Remove the pan from the heat.

Place the shallots or onions, apples and vinegar in a heavy-bottomed, nonreactive skillet and cook them over medium heat until the vinegar has evaporated and the shallots or onions are limp — about two minutes. Add the beef and brown it over high heat, breaking up any whole pieces as you do so. Remove the skillet from the heat and stir in the thyme, some pepper and the thickened stock.

Divide the meat mixture evenly among four small gratin dishes or place it in one large dish. Top the meat with the potato mixture, smooth the surface with a spatula, and flute the potatoes using the edge of the spatula. Brush the surface with the remaining 2 teaspoons of oil. Bake the beef and potatoes until the potatoes are lightly browned — 20 to 30 minutes.

SUGGESTED ACCOMPANIMENT: *Bibb lettuce and radish salad.*

Ground Beef with Peppers and Pasta

Serves 6
Working (and total) time: about 30 minutes

Calories **415**
Protein **28g.**
Cholesterol **50mg.**
Total fat **9g.**
Saturated fat **3g.**
Sodium **260mg.**

1¼ lb. beef round, trimmed of fat and ground (box, page 8)
2 sweet red peppers
1 tbsp. olive oil
2 onions, finely chopped
1 tsp. fennel seeds
6 garlic cloves, thinly sliced
1 tsp. salt
freshly ground black pepper
14 oz. canned unsalted whole tomatoes, drained, seeded and chopped, the juice reserved
⅓ cup red wine vinegar
1 tsp. sugar
2 zucchini (about ¾ lb.), trimmed, halved lengthwise and cut on the diagonal into ¼-inch pieces
¾ lb. penne or other tubular pasta
1 cup unsalted chicken stock (recipe, page 137)
½ cup tightly packed fresh basil, shredded
¼ cup freshly grated Parmesan cheese

Roast the peppers about 2 inches below a preheated broiler, turning them every now and then until their skin becomes blistered. Transfer the peppers to a bowl and cover it with plastic wrap; the trapped steam will loosen their skin. When the peppers are cool, peel, seed and derib them, holding them over a bowl to catch any juice. Cut the peppers into thin strips and strain the juice to remove any seeds. Set the strips and juice aside.

While the peppers are roasting, heat the oil in a heavy-bottomed skillet over medium-high heat. Add the ground beef, onions, fennel seeds, garlic, ¼ teaspoon of the salt and some pepper. Cook the mixture, stirring frequently, until the beef begins to brown. Add the tomatoes and their juice, the vinegar and the sugar. Reduce the heat to medium low and simmer the mixture for 10 minutes. Add the zucchini and the peppers and their juice; cook the mixture for another five minutes.

Meanwhile, add the pasta and the remaining ¾ teaspoon salt to 3 quarts of boiling water; cook the pasta for six minutes — it will be underdone. Drain the pasta and return it to the pot; pour in the stock, cover the pot and slowly bring the stock to a simmer. Cook the pasta for one minute longer, then add the beef mixture, the basil and a liberal grinding of pepper, and stir well. Simmer the mixture, stirring frequently, until most of the liquid is absorbed — two to three minutes.

Transfer the beef and pasta to a large bowl. Sprinkle the Parmesan cheese over the top and serve at once.

SUGGESTED ACCOMPANIMENT: *arugula or other salad greens.*

Spicy Ground Meat on a Bed of Sweet Potatoes

Serves 4
Working time: about 1 hour
Total time: about 2 hours and 30 minutes

Calories **522**
Protein **35g.**
Cholesterol **73mg.**
Total fat **10g.**
Saturated fat **3g.**
Sodium **260mg.**

1¼ lb. beef round, trimmed of fat and ground (box, page 8)
4 sweet potatoes (about 2¼ lb.)
3 lb. ripe tomatoes, chopped
2 bay leaves
2 cinnamon sticks
4 allspice berries
8 black peppercorns
2 dried red chili peppers, or ¼ tsp. cayenne pepper
1 tbsp. tomato paste
1 tsp. safflower oil
1 onion, finely chopped
¼ tsp. salt
2 tbsp. chopped fresh parsley
½ cup low-fat yogurt

Preheat the oven to 400° F. Bake the sweet potatoes for one hour or until they are tender when pierced with the tip of a sharp knife.

Meanwhile, put the tomatoes, bay leaves, cinnamon sticks, allspice berries, peppercorns, and chili peppers or cayenne pepper into a heavy-bottomed, nonreactive pan. Bring the mixture to a boil, then reduce the heat to medium low, and simmer it uncovered, stirring frequently, until it is reduced to 2 cups — about one hour and 30 minutes. Remove the cinnamon sticks and bay leaves from the tomato sauce, discard them, and put the sauce through a food mill. Set the sauce aside.

Sauté the beef in a large, nonstick skillet over high heat, breaking it into chunks as it cooks. When the beef is evenly browned — about five minutes — add the tomato sauce and the tomato paste. Simmer the meat, partially covered to prevent splattering, until most of the liquid has evaporated — about 20 minutes. Pour the meat sauce into a bowl and keep it warm.

Peel the baked sweet potatoes and chop them coarsely. Wipe out the skillet with a paper towel, pour in the oil and heat it over low heat. Add the onion and cook it until it is translucent — about five minutes. Add the sweet potatoes and ¼ cup of water, and cook the mixture, stirring frequently, over medium heat until the water is absorbed — about five minutes; stir in the salt and chopped parsley.

Place the sweet potatoes on a serving platter and top them with the meat. Serve immediately, passing the yogurt separately.

SUGGESTED ACCOMPANIMENT: *steamed snow peas.*

Bulgur-Stuffed Red Peppers

Serves 4
Working time: about 25 minutes
Total time: about 45 minutes

Calories **285**
Protein **20g.**
Cholesterol **40mg.**
Total fat **9g.**
Saturated fat **2g.**
Sodium **210mg.**

¾ lb. beef round, trimmed of fat and ground (box, page 8)
4 large sweet red or green peppers
4 tsp. olive oil
1 onion, chopped
2 tsp. fresh thyme, or ½ tsp. dried thyme leaves
¼ lb. mushrooms, wiped clean and thinly sliced (about 1¼ cups)
2 tbsp. finely chopped celery
¾ cup bulgur
¼ tsp. salt
freshly ground black pepper
1½ cups unsalted brown stock or unsalted chicken stock (recipes, page 137)
1 garlic clove, finely chopped
2 tbsp. sherry vinegar or red wine vinegar

Preheat the oven to 400° F.

To prepare the peppers, cut out and discard their stems. Slice off the peppers' tops, dice them, and set the pieces aside. Seed and derib the peppers.

Heat 1 tablespoon of the oil in a heavy-bottomed saucepan over medium heat. Add half of the onion, half of the thyme, the mushrooms, celery, bulgur, ⅛ teaspoon of the salt and some pepper. Cook the vegetables and bulgur, stirring frequently, for five minutes. Add the stock, stir the mixture well, and cover the pan. Cook the mixture, stirring it occasionally, until the liquid is absorbed — about 12 minutes.

In a nonstick skillet, heat the remaining teaspoon of oil over medium-high heat. When the skillet is hot, add the beef, the reserved diced peppers, the remaining onion, the remaining thyme and the garlic. Cook, stirring frequently, until the beef is browned — five to seven minutes. Add the remaining ⅛ teaspoon of salt, some pepper and the vinegar. Cook the mixture for 30 seconds, then remove it from the heat.

Combine the bulgur mixture with the beef and fill the peppers, mounding the filling. Bake the stuffed peppers in a shallow casserole, loosely covered with aluminum foil, for 25 minutes. Allow the peppers to stand for five minutes before serving them.

SUGGESTED ACCOMPANIMENT: *cucumber and onion salad.*

one hour and 30 minutes. If the tomato sauce begins to scorch, stir about ½ cup of water into it.

While the meat is cooking, make the cabbage slaw. Toss the cabbage in a bowl with the carrot, apple, yogurt, mustard, horseradish, salt and celery seeds. Cover the bowl and refrigerate it.

When the meat is done, remove it from the saucepan and let it sit at room temperature. Add the celery leaves, lemon juice, brown sugar, hot red-pepper sauce, salt and some pepper to the tomato mixture. Coarsely chop the beef and add it also. Simmer the barbecue beef over low heat for 30 minutes.

Split the rolls and fill them with the beef, topped with some of the cabbage slaw.

Beef Barbecue Sandwiches

Serves 8
Working time: about 45 minutes
Total time: about 2 hours and 30 minutes

Calories **380**
Protein **34g.**
Cholesterol **87mg.**
Total fat **10g.**
Saturated fat **3g.**
Sodium **435mg.**

one 2½ lb. arm pot roast, trimmed of fat
28 oz. canned unsalted whole tomatoes, puréed in a food processor or a blender, and sieved
1 onion, finely chopped
¾ cup cider vinegar
½ cup finely chopped celery leaves
juice of 1 lemon
¼ cup light brown sugar
10 drops hot red-pepper sauce
¼ tsp. salt
freshly ground black pepper
8 kaiser rolls
Cabbage slaw
½ small head of cabbage, shredded (about 4 cups)
1 small carrot, grated
1 red apple, grated
1 cup low-fat yogurt
½ tsp. dry mustard
1 tsp. prepared horseradish
¼ tsp. salt
½ tsp. celery seeds

Pour the puréed tomatoes into a large saucepan along with 3 cups of water. Add the onion, vinegar and beef, and bring the liquid to a simmer over medium heat. Reduce the heat, cover the pan, leaving the lid slightly ajar, and simmer the mixture, stirring occasionally, for

Spicy Ground Beef Baked in Corn Bread

Serves 4
Working time: about 25 minutes
Total time: about 1 hour

Calories **395**
Protein **28g.**
Cholesterol **56mg.**
Total fat **10g.**
Saturated fat **3g.**
Sodium **325mg.**

1 lb. beef round, trimmed of fat, ground (box, page 8), and crumbled into small pieces
1 onion, chopped
½ green pepper, seeded, deribbed and diced
3 garlic cloves, thinly sliced
1 tsp. chili powder
1 tsp. dry mustard
¼ tsp. cayenne pepper
14 oz. canned unsalted whole tomatoes, drained
1 tsp. sugar
⅓ cup red wine vinegar
⅛ tsp. salt
Corn bread
⅔ cup yellow stone-ground cornmeal
⅔ cup unbleached all-purpose flour
1 tbsp. sugar
1½ tsp. baking powder
½ tsp. chili powder
1 tbsp. safflower oil
¾ cup low-fat milk
1 egg white

Heat a large, nonstick skillet over medium-high heat. Combine the beef, onion, green pepper, garlic, chili powder, mustard and cayenne pepper in the skillet. Stir the mixture frequently, until the beef is cooked through — four to five minutes. Add the tomatoes, sugar, vinegar and salt, crushing the tomatoes; cook the mixture until most of the liquid has evaporated — 15 to 20 minutes. Set it aside.

Preheat the oven to 450° F.

To make the corn bread, sift the cornmeal, flour, sugar, baking powder and chili powder into a bowl. Add the oil, stir well, and work the oil into the dry ingredients with your fingertips until no lumps remain; the mixture will be very dry. In a separate bowl, whisk the milk and the egg white together, and add the liquid to the cornmeal mixture. Stir gently just to incorporate the liquid; do not overmix.

Lightly oil a 1½-quart baking dish. Pour the corn-bread batter into the dish. Spoon the beef and vegetables into the center of the batter, leaving a 1½-inch border all around. Bake the mixture for 25 minutes. Remove the dish from the oven and let it stand for five minutes before serving.

SUGGESTED ACCOMPANIMENT: *red pepper and scallion salad.*

2 *Skewers threaded with lamb, onions, peppers and apples will be quickly grilled and served with a sauce of black olives and mint (recipe, page 84).*

Discovering Delicious Lamb

Lamb looms big in the cuisines of many cultures, but curiously not the American. The succulent cooking of the Middle East, for one, is based largely on lamb, with dishes ranging from kebabs to the whole animal spit-roasted over a charcoal fire. America's hesitation to put lamb regularly on its tables is at last changing, and this section demonstrates, through its 38 recipes, just how delicious lamb can be.

Lamb's growing popularity has partly to do with the greater sophistication of today's cooks, who are willing to experiment more, and thereby widen their culinary horizons with a meat that has a rich, satisfying flavor all its own. And it has also to do with the fact that lamb comes from a young animal, which means that invariably the meat will be tender and — perhaps more to the point in a book like this — that it will have relatively little fat within its muscle tissue. What visible fat there is can be easily trimmed.

Although lamb by nature is not fatty meat, it nevertheless has a varying fat content in its different parts, and thus cuts that have 45 percent or more of their calories in fat have been excluded. Among these are cuts from the shoulder, rib and breast. Also omitted are lamb variety meats, such as tongue, which is high in fat, and the kidneys, which are high in cholesterol.

For such a small animal, lamb still offers a full range of acceptable cuts and cooking possibilities. In purchasing lamb, select meat that is pinkish-red in color and that has a velvety appearance where the flesh lies exposed. The leg alone can be prepared whole, boned, stuffed and rolled, butterflied or cut into steaks, all of which are done in this section. The leg meat may even be ground and used in as many ways as ground beef — and then some.

Lamb Scallopini with Mustard and Tarragon

Serves 4
Working (and total) time: about 20 minutes

Calories **225**
Protein **26g.**
Cholesterol **78mg.**
Total fat **12g.**
Saturated fat **4g.**
Sodium **190mg.**

8 lamb scallopini (about 1 lb.), cut from the sirloin
2 tbsp. Dijon mustard
1 tbsp. olive oil
½ cup dry bread crumbs
1 tbsp. chopped fresh tarragon, or 1 tsp. dried tarragon
2 tbsp. chopped fresh parsley
freshly ground black pepper
4 lemon wedges for garnish
4 parsley sprigs for garnish

Preheat the broiler. Place each lamb slice between two sheets of plastic wrap or wax paper, and pound the slices with a meat mallet or the flat of a heavy knife until they are very thin.

Combine the mustard and oil in a small bowl. In a second bowl, mix together the bread crumbs, tarragon, parsley and pepper. Sprinkle the bread-crumb mixture onto a large sheet of wax paper. Brush one side of a lamb slice to coat it lightly with the mustard-oil mixture; set the slice mustard side down on the crumbs. Brush the second side with the mustard-oil mixture and turn the slice to coat it thoroughly with the crumbs. Repeat the process to coat the remaining slices of lamb.

Transfer the lamb slices to a baking sheet and sprinkle any remaining crumbs over them. Broil the scallopini until they are golden brown — two to three minutes per side. Garnish each portion with a lemon wedge and a parsley sprig just before serving.

SUGGESTED ACCOMPANIMENT: *broiled vegetable kebabs.*

Spiced Lamb Chops with Green-Tomato Chutney

Serves 4
Working time: about 45 minutes
Total time: about 2 hours and 15 minutes
(includes marinating)

Calories **295**
Protein **25g.**
Cholesterol **73mg.**
Total fat **9g.**
Saturated fat **3g.**
Sodium **205mg.**

4 lamb sirloin chops (about 5 oz. each), trimmed of fat
1 onion, finely chopped
½ cup red wine vinegar
¼ cup dark brown sugar
1 tbsp. dry mustard
½ tsp. ground allspice
½ tsp. ground ginger
½ tsp. ground cinnamon
2 scallions, trimmed and thinly sliced

Green-tomato chutney

2 green tomatoes, finely chopped
2 tart green apples, cored and chopped
¼ tsp. salt
freshly ground black pepper

Mix the onion, vinegar, sugar, mustard, allspice, ginger and cinnamon in a small bowl. Place the chops in a shallow dish and pour the marinade over them. Let the chops marinate at room temperature for one hour.

If you plan to grill the lamb, prepare the coals about 30 minutes before cooking time; to broil, preheat the broiler for 10 minutes.

At the end of the marinating time, remove the chops from the marinade and refrigerate the meat. To make the chutney, pour the marinade into a nonreactive saucepan set over medium-low heat. Add the tomatoes, apples, salt and some pepper to the marinade, and bring the mixture to a simmer. Cook the chutney, uncovered, for 15 minutes, then partly cover the saucepan, and continue cooking the chutney until it is quite thick — about 15 minutes more.

Spread the chutney on a serving platter and sprinkle the scallions over it. Cook the chops for about two minutes on each side for medium-rare meat. Arrange the chops atop the chutney and serve them at once.

SUGGESTED ACCOMPANIMENT: *steamed broccoli with oven-baked potato slices.*

Gyros

TRADITIONAL FARE IN GREEK NEIGHBORHOODS,
GYROS IS MADE UP OF LAYERS OF MEAT AND HERBS.
THE ACCOMPANYING TZATZIKI IS A YOGURT SAUCE SEASONED
WITH CUCUMBER AND DILL.

Serves 12
Working time: about 45 minutes
Total time: about 2 hours (includes marinating)

Calories **340**
Protein **33g.**
Cholesterol **78mg.**
Total fat **10g.**
Saturated fat **3g.**
Sodium **205mg.**

2½ lb. boneless leg of lamb, trimmed of fat
1 lb. beef eye round, trimmed of fat
juice of 1 lemon
3 garlic cloves, finely chopped
3 tbsp. finely chopped fresh oregano, or 1 tbsp. dried oregano
½ tsp. ground coriander
½ tsp. salt
freshly ground black pepper
2 egg whites
½ tbsp. paprika, preferably Hungarian
1 tbsp. safflower oil
12 pita breads, cut in half
1 head of romaine lettuce, shredded
3 large ripe tomatoes, chopped

Tzatziki

1 cup plain low-fat yogurt
1 cucumber, peeled, halved and seeded
¼ cup loosely packed fresh dill, finely cut, or 3 tbsp. chopped fresh parsley mixed with 1 tbsp. dried dill
½ tsp. distilled white vinegar
⅛ tsp. salt

Cut the lamb against the grain into thin slices. Place the lamb slices between two sheets of plastic wrap or wax paper, and pound the meat with a mallet or the flat of a heavy knife to a thickness of about ⅛ inch. Transfer the lamb slices to a bowl.

    Cut the beef against the grain into slices about ¼

inch thick. Pound the slices as you did the lamb and transfer them to a second bowl.

In a small bowl, stir together the lemon juice, garlic, oregano, coriander, salt and some pepper. Divide this mixture between the beef and lamb slices, and toss them in their separate bowls to distribute the seasonings evenly. In another small bowl, lightly beat the egg whites with the paprika.

To assemble the gyros, brush a slice of beef with some of the egg-white mixture and set the slice on a clean work surface. Top the beef with two slices of lamb and brush them with the egg-white mixture, too. Continue stacking and brushing the beef and lamb slices, ending with a slice of beef. Press down on the stack to compact it, forcing out any excess liquid. Insert a long metal skewer through the stack, slightly off center. Lay the stack on its side and thread a second skewer through the meat from the other end. Let the gyros stand at room temperature for one to two hours before grilling it.

Purée the tzatziki ingredients in a food processor or a blender. Transfer the sauce to a bowl and chill it.

About 30 minutes before cooking time, light the coals in an outdoor grill. When the coals are hot, bank them against the sides of the grill. Place a foil drip pan in the center of the grate and set the rack in place. Brush the gyros with the oil and lay it on the center of the rack. Grill the gyros, turning it often to ensure that it cooks evenly — about 30 minutes for medium meat, or until an instant-reading meat thermometer inserted in the center registers 150° F.

Remove the gyros from the grill and let it stand for 10 minutes before removing the skewers. With a very sharp knife, cut the meat lengthwise into thin slices. Fill the pita pockets with the meat, lettuce, tomato and tzatziki sauce. Serve immediately.

SUGGESTED ACCOMPANIMENT: *pickled hot peppers.*

Marinated Lamb with Spiced Apple Butter

Serves 12
Working time: about 30 minutes
Total time: about 1 hour and 30 minutes

Calories **175**
Protein **19g.**
Cholesterol **62mg.**
Total fat **7g.**
Saturated fat **2g.**
Sodium **140mg.**

one 5-lb. leg of lamb, trimmed of fat and boned (technique, page 105)
½ cup apple butter
¼ cup cider vinegar
1 onion, finely chopped
2 garlic cloves, finely chopped
1 tbsp. finely chopped fresh sage, or 1½ tsp. dried sage
½ tsp. salt
1 tbsp. freshly ground black pepper
1 tbsp. safflower oil

Spread the boned leg of lamb flat on a work surface with the cut side of the meat facing up. Cut out the membranes and tendons and discard them. Slice horizontally into — but not completely through — the thick section of flesh at one side of the leg and open out the resulting flap. Then slice and open out the opposite side in a similar manner. The meat should be no more than 2 inches thick.

Mix the apple butter, vinegar, onion, garlic, sage, salt, pepper and oil in a large bowl. Put the butterflied lamb into the bowl and slather it all over with the spiced apple butter. Leave the lamb in the bowl to marinate at room temperature for one hour, turning it after 30 minutes.

If you plan to grill the lamb, prepare the coals about 30 minutes before grilling time; to broil, preheat the broiler for 10 minutes. Remove the lamb from the marinade, holding it over the bowl to allow any excess marinade to drip off. Reserve the marinade.

Cook the lamb for 10 minutes on each side for medium-rare meat. Baste the lamb from time to time with the reserved marinade.

Let the lamb rest for 15 minutes before carving it.

SUGGESTED ACCOMPANIMENTS: *steamed zucchini; baked sweet potatoes.*

Lamb Kebabs with Olive-Mint Sauce

Serves 4
Working time: about 25 minutes
Total time: about 40 minutes

Calories **240**
Protein **24g.**
Cholesterol **75mg.**
Total fat **12g.**
Saturated fat **3g.**
Sodium **295mg.**

1 ¼ lb. lean lamb (from the sirloin), trimmed of fat and cut into 16 cubes
½ cup chopped fresh mint
6 oil-cured black olives, pitted and finely chopped
1 tbsp. olive oil
½ tsp. ground allspice
freshly ground black pepper
2 onions, each one cut into 6 wedges
½ green pepper, seeded, deribbed and cut into 8 pieces
½ red apple, cored and cut into 8 pieces
1 cup unsalted brown stock or unsalted chicken stock (recipes, page 137)
⅛ tsp. salt

If you plan to grill the lamb, prepare the coals about 30 minutes before cooking time; to broil, preheat the broiler for 10 minutes.

Put the lamb cubes into a bowl along with 3 tablespoons of the mint, half of the olives, ½ tablespoon of the oil, ¼ teaspoon of the allspice and a generous grinding of pepper. Stir the lamb cubes to coat them with the marinade and set the bowl aside at room temperature while you prepare the other ingredients.

Gently toss together the onions, green pepper, apple, 3 tablespoons of the remaining mint, the remaining ½ tablespoon of olive oil, the remaining ¼ teaspoon of ground allspice and some pepper in another bowl, and set it aside.

Pour the stock into a small saucepan over medium heat, then stir in the remaining olives, the remaining 2 tablespoons of mint and the salt. Cook the sauce until only about ⅓ cup remains — about 10 minutes. Remove the pan from the heat and set it aside.

Thread the lamb cubes and the vegetable and apple chunks onto four skewers.

Grill or broil the kebabs for three to four minutes per side for medium meat. Transfer them to a platter. Reheat the sauce, pour it over the kebabs, and serve them immediately.

SUGGESTED ACCOMPANIMENT: *lentil and onion salad.*

Lamb Sausages on Skewers

Serves 4
Working time: about 30 minutes
Total time: about 1 hour

Calories **245**	
Protein **26g.**	1¼ lb. lean lamb (from the leg or loin), trimmed of fat and ground (box, page 8)
Cholesterol **77mg.**	1 large ripe tomato, seeded and chopped
Total fat **11g.**	¼ tsp. salt
Saturated fat **4g.**	freshly ground black pepper
Sodium **320mg.**	1 tsp. sugar
	1 tbsp. red wine vinegar
	3 tbsp. chopped fresh parsley
	1 tbsp. chopped fresh oregano, or 1 tsp. dried oregano
	1 egg white
	1 tbsp. olive oil
	⅓ cup dry bread crumbs
	2 scallions, trimmed and thinly sliced
	½ tsp. capers, rinsed
	½ cup plain low-fat yogurt

Put the tomato, ⅛ teaspoon of the salt, some pepper, the sugar and the vinegar into a heavy-bottomed skillet set over medium heat. Cook the mixture, stirring frequently, until only about ¼ cup remains — approximately 20 minutes. Transfer the mixture to a bowl and refrigerate it until it has cooled.

In a large bowl, combine the ground lamb with 2 tablespoons of the parsley, the oregano, egg white, ½ tablespoon of the oil, the bread crumbs, half of the scallions, the remaining ⅛ teaspoon of salt and some pepper. Stir the cooled tomato mixture into the lamb mixture and refrigerate the bowl until the contents are thoroughly chilled — about 30 minutes.

If you plan to grill the sausages, prepare the coals about 30 minutes before cooking time; to broil, preheat the broiler for 10 minutes.

Divide the sausage mixture into four parts and form each one into a cylinder about 4 inches long. Thread each cylinder onto a skewer, keeping the meat pressed firmly in place.

Pour the remaining ½ tablespoon of oil onto a large, flat plate. Lightly coat the sausages by rolling them in the oil. Grill or broil the sausages, turning the skewers every now and then, until the meat is lightly browned — eight to 10 minutes.

Meanwhile, finely chop the remaining tablespoon of parsley, the remaining scallions and the capers. Transfer the chopped parsley mixture to a small bowl and whisk in the yogurt and some pepper. Serve the sausages immediately, passing the sauce separately.

SUGGESTED ACCOMPANIMENT: *couscous tossed with cinnamon and grated carrots.*

30 minutes before cooking time; to broil, preheat the broiler for 10 minutes.

To make the chutney glaze, combine the stock and the chutney in a small saucepan and bring the mixture to a simmer over medium heat. Stir the mustard and the vinegar into the cornstarch paste and then whisk this mixture into the simmering stock and chutney. Cook the glaze, stirring continuously, until it thickens — about one minute.

With your fingers, rub both sides of the lamb with the oil. Cook the lamb, turning it every five minutes, until it is well browned on both sides — about 20 minutes in all. Sprinkle the salt and some pepper on the lamb and brush it with some of the chutney glaze. Continue cooking the lamb, turning and basting it frequently with the glaze for 10 minutes more.

Transfer the lamb to a cutting board and sprinkle it with the chopped mint. Allow the meat to stand for 10 minutes before carving it. Serve the lamb in slices, accompanied by the remaining chutney glaze and garnished with mint sprigs.

SUGGESTED ACCOMPANIMENT: *a salad of bulgur and tomatoes.*

Grilled Lamb with Chutney Glaze and Mint

Serves 10
Working time: about 30 minutes
Total time: about 1 hour and 15 minutes

Calories **200**
Protein **23g.**
Cholesterol **75mg.**
Total fat **8g.**
Saturated fat **3g.**
Sodium **135mg.**

one 5-lb. leg of lamb, trimmed of fat and boned (technique, page 105)
1 tbsp. safflower oil
¼ tsp. salt
freshly ground black pepper
4 tbsp. chopped fresh mint, or 4 tsp. dried mint
several fresh mint sprigs, for garnish
Chutney glaze
1 cup unsalted brown stock or unsalted chicken stock (recipes, page 137)
¼ cup mango chutney
½ tbsp. dry mustard
1 tbsp. cider vinegar
½ tbsp. cornstarch, mixed with 1 tbsp. water

Spread the boned leg of lamb flat on a work surface with the cut side of the meat facing up. Cut out the membranes and tendons and discard them. Slice horizontally into — but not completely through — the thick section of flesh at one side of the leg and open out the resulting flap. Then slice and open out the opposite side in a similar manner. The meat should be no more than 2 inches thick.

If you plan to grill the lamb, prepare the coals about

Sweet and Spicy Grilled Lamb

Serves 4
Working time: about 1 hour
Total time: about 2 hours (includes marinating)

Calories **310**
Protein **23g.**
Cholesterol **68mg.**
Total fat **8g.**
Saturated fat **3g.**
Sodium **205mg.**

one 2½-lb. lamb loin roast, trimmed of fat and boned (technique, page 89)
freshly ground black pepper
¼ tsp. ground allspice
¼ tsp. ground cloves
2 tbsp. fresh lemon juice
2 tbsp. light brown sugar
Cherry ketchup
1½ cups sweet cherries, stemmed and pitted
¼ cup light brown sugar
¼ tsp. salt
6 tbsp. cider vinegar
one 3-inch strip of lemon zest
½ tsp. ground ginger
2 cinnamon sticks
⅛ tsp. cayenne pepper

To make the ketchup, combine the cherries, brown sugar, salt, vinegar, lemon zest, ginger, cinnamon sticks and cayenne pepper in a heavy-bottomed saucepan. Bring the mixture to a simmer and cook it until it has thickened — about 15 minutes. Discard the cinnamon sticks and pour the mixture into a food processor or a blender. Purée the mixture, then strain it into a small bowl. Refrigerate the ketchup.

To prepare the marinade, mix a generous grinding of pepper with the allspice, cloves, lemon juice and brown sugar in a small bowl. Set the loin in a shallow dish and pour the marinade over it, rubbing the spices into the meat. Let the loin marinate at room temperature for one hour, turning it every 15 minutes.

If you plan to grill the meat, prepare the coals about 30 minutes before cooking time; to broil, preheat the broiler for about 10 minutes. Remove the loin from the marinade and cook it for five minutes on each side, brushing it occasionally with any marinade remaining in the dish. Let the lamb rest for five minutes before slicing it. Pass the ketchup separately.

SUGGESTED ACCOMPANIMENT: *steamed cauliflower*.

Loin of Lamb Stuffed with Wild Mushrooms

Serves 4
Working time: about 1 hour
Total time: about 1 hour and 45 minutes

Calories **235**
Protein **24g.**
Cholesterol **69mg.**
Total fat **11g.**
Saturated fat **4g.**
Sodium **225mg.**

2½ lb. lamb loin roast, trimmed of fat and boned (technique, page 89)	
1 oz. dried wild mushrooms (chanterelle, porcini or shiitake), soaked in 1 cup very hot water for 20 minutes	
1 tbsp. olive oil	
3 scallions, the white parts finely chopped, the green tops cut into 1-inch pieces	
1 tbsp. finely chopped celery	
2 garlic cloves, finely chopped	
2 tsp. fresh thyme, or ¾ tsp. dried thyme leaves	
¼ lb. fresh mushrooms, wiped clean and chopped	
1 cup unsalted brown stock (recipe, page 137)	
1 tbsp. fresh lemon juice	
¼ tsp. salt	
freshly ground black pepper	

Remove the dried mushrooms from their soaking liquid and cut off any woody or sandy stems. Finely chop the mushrooms and set them aside. Carefully pour the soaking liquid through a cheesecloth-lined sieve set over a bowl to strain out any grit. Set the bowl aside.

Heat ½ tablespoon of the oil in a heavy-bottomed saucepan over medium heat. Add the white parts of the scallions, the celery, garlic and half of the thyme. Cook the mixture, stirring occasionally, for three minutes. Add all the mushrooms to the pan along with ¼ cup of the stock, the lemon juice, ⅛ teaspoon of the salt and a generous grinding of pepper. Cover the pan, reduce the heat to low, and cook the mushrooms, stirring them every now and then, until all the liquid has been absorbed — 20 to 25 minutes. Transfer the mushroom stuffing to a bowl; refrigerate the stuffing until it has reached room temperature.

Preheat the oven to 425° F. To butterfly the loin and prepare it for stuffing, cut the meat in half horizontally, leaving the halves hinged at one side. Open out the meat and spread the stuffing down the center of it. Fold the halves back together and tie the roast securely (technique, page 25). Place the roast in a heavy-bottomed roasting pan and brush it with the remaining ½ tablespoon of oil. Roast the loin for about 25 minutes or until a thermometer inserted in the meat registers 150° F. for medium.

Remove the pan from the oven and set the roast aside on a cutting board while you prepare the sauce. Discard the fat from the pan, leaving behind any caramelized juices. Place the pan over medium heat. Pour the strained mushroom liquid and the remaining ¾ cup of stock into the pan, stirring well with a wooden spoon to dissolve the caramelized juices in the bottom. Stir in the remaining ⅛ teaspoon of salt, the remaining thyme, the scallion tops and some pepper. Boil the liquid until about ½ cup of sauce remains — approximately 10 minutes.

Cut the loin into 12 slices and arrange them on a platter or on individual plates. Pour the sauce over the slices and serve them immediately.

SUGGESTED ACCOMPANIMENTS: *green peas; French bread.*

Boning a Loin of Lamb

1 *REMOVING THE EXCESS FAT. A loin roast is generally sold with an apron — or extra flap of fatty meat — attached to it. Cut off the flap where it joins the loin. Discard the flap.*

2 *STARTING THE BONING. With the fatty layer of the loin roast facing up, insert the tip of a boning knife between the meat and the backbone, and use short slicing strokes to separate one from the other.*

3 *REMOVING THE LOIN. Carefully pulling away the meat with one hand, continue cutting along the ribs until the meat is freed. Set the loin aside.*

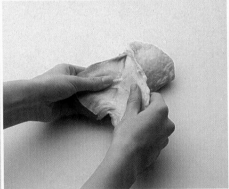

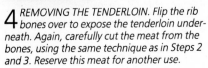

4 *REMOVING THE TENDERLOIN. Flip the rib bones over to expose the tenderloin underneath. Again, carefully cut the meat from the bones, using the same technique as in Steps 2 and 3. Reserve this meat for another use.*

5 *PEELING OFF THE FATTY LAYER. Pick up the loin in your hands and remove the thick, white layer of fat from the meat by gently pulling it off. If this is done carefully, the whole layer should come away in one piece.*

6 *STRIPPING OFF THE SILVER SKIN. With the knife tip, cut under the whitish membrane to form a tab. Pull the tab taut and insert the knife under it. Cut toward yourself to remove a strip of the silver skin; remove the remainder in the same way.*

Garlic-Studded Lamb Shanks with Roasted Onions

Serves 4
Working time: about 20 minutes
Total time: about 2 hours

Calories **285**
Protein **31g.**
Cholesterol **86mg.**
Total fat **9g.**
Saturated fat **3g.**
Sodium **290mg.**

4 lamb shanks (about ¾ lb. each), trimmed of fat
6 garlic cloves, each cut lengthwise into 4 slices
½ tbsp. olive oil
1 tbsp. finely chopped fresh rosemary, or ½ tbsp. dried rosemary
freshly ground black pepper
¼ tsp. salt
4 onions, unpeeled
6 carrots, cut into bâtonnets and blanched for 1 minute in boiling water

Preheat the oven to 350° F.

With the point of a knife, make an incision in the flesh of a shank; press a garlic slice deep into the open-ing. Repeat the process to insert six garlic slices into each shank. Rub the shanks with the oil, then sprinkle them with the rosemary and pepper. Put the shanks in a heavy-bottomed roasting pan and bake them until they are very tender — one and a half to two hours.

After the lamb shanks have been baking for 45 minutes, sprinkle them with the salt. Wrap the onions individually in aluminum foil and set them in the oven next to the roasting pan.

When the shanks are done, transfer them to a serving platter. Discard the fat that has collected in the roasting pan, leaving any caramelized juices in the pan. Set the pan on the stove top over medium heat. Add the blanched carrot sticks and cook them, stirring occasionally, for two minutes. Pour ¼ cup of water into the pan and bring the liquid to a simmer, scraping up the caramelized pan juices with a wooden spoon.

Transfer the carrots and the sauce to the platter. Unwrap the onions, cut off ½ inch from their tops and set them on the platter just before serving.

SUGGESTED ACCOMPANIMENTS: *escarole; Italian bread.*

Stuffed Lamb Chops

Serves 4
Working time: about 20 minutes
Total time: about 40 minutes

Calories **235**
Protein **21g.**
Cholesterol **59mg.**
Total fat **12g.**
Saturated fat **3g.**
Sodium **230mg.**

four 4-oz. lamb loin chops, trimmed of fat
1 tbsp. safflower oil
½ cup chopped onion
½ cup unsalted chicken stock (recipe, page 137)
3 tbsp. currants
½ cup fresh bread crumbs
2 tsp. chopped fresh parsley
2 tbsp. finely chopped walnuts
1 tsp. fresh thyme, or ¼ tsp. dried thyme leaves
¼ tsp. salt
freshly ground black pepper

To prepare the stuffing, heat ½ tablespoon of the oil in a nonstick skillet over medium heat. Add the onion and cook it until it is translucent — about three minutes. Add the stock and currants and bring the liquid to a simmer. Remove the skillet from the heat and cover it. Let the mixture stand until the currants have plumped — about five minutes. Stir in the bread crumbs, parsley, walnuts, thyme, ⅛ teaspoon of the salt and some pepper, and set the stuffing aside.

Preheat the oven to 350° F. Using the technique on page 25, step 1, cut a pocket in each lamb chop. With a spoon or your fingers, fill the pockets with the stuffing. Heat the remaining ½ tablespoon of oil in an oven-proof skillet over medium-high heat. Place the stuffed chops in the oil and lightly brown them on the first side — one to two minutes. Turn the chops over and season them with the remaining ⅛ teaspoon of salt and some more pepper. Put the skillet into the oven and bake the chops for 10 to 12 minutes. Remove the skillet from the oven and let the chops rest for five minutes before serving them.

SUGGESTED ACCOMPANIMENT: *baked butternut squash.*

vinegar, mirin or sherry, and pepper in a small bowl. Pour the marinade over the lamb and refrigerate it for at least three hours, or as long as overnight. From time to time, baste the lamb with the marinade.

Toward the end of the marinating time, preheat the oven to 450° F. Transfer the lamb to a roasting pan, reserving the marinade, and roast the lamb for 15 minutes. Reduce the oven temperature to 325° F. and continue roasting the lamb, basting it occasionally with the reserved marinade, until a meat thermometer inserted in the center registers 140° F. — about 50 minutes more. Let the lamb rest for 20 minutes before carving it.

While the lamb is resting, combine the dipping-sauce ingredients. Serve the dipping sauce at room temperature with the lamb slices.

SUGGESTED ACCOMPANIMENT: *a cold salad of Asian noodles.*

Leg of Lamb Roasted with Ginger

Serves 10
Working time: about 25 minutes
Total time: about 4 hours and 30 minutes
(includes marinating)

Calories **185**
Protein **24g.**
Cholesterol **75mg.**
Total fat **7g.**
Saturated fat **3g.**
Sodium **170mg.**

one 5-lb. leg of lamb, trimmed of fat
3 tbsp. finely chopped fresh ginger
3 garlic cloves, finely chopped
2 tsp. low-sodium soy sauce
¼ tsp. dark sesame oil
1 tsp. rice vinegar or distilled white vinegar
⅓ cup mirin (sweetened Japanese rice wine) or sweet sherry
⅛ tsp. white pepper
Dipping sauce
1 tbsp. low-sodium soy sauce
2 tbsp. mirin or sweet sherry
1 tsp. sesame seeds
2 tsp. rice vinegar or distilled white vinegar
1 scallion, trimmed and thinly sliced
1 small carrot, sliced into thin rounds
2 tbsp. chopped fresh ginger
½ cup unsalted brown stock or unsalted chicken stock (recipes, page 137)

With a knife, lightly score the surface of the lamb in a crosshatch pattern. Transfer the lamb to a shallow baking dish. Mix the ginger, garlic, soy sauce, sesame oil,

How to Carve a Roast Leg of Lamb

1 *CARVING THE OUTER SIDE. With the meatier portion of the leg facing up, grip the shank end with a towel and tilt the roast. Holding the roast firmly and cutting away from yourself, carve the meat at an angle, against the grain, in thin slices.*

2 *CARVING THE INNER SIDE. After you have finished slicing the meat from the rounded side, rotate the leg of lamb so you can get at the other meaty portion. Again, carve the lamb at an angle, against the grain, into thin slices.*

Lamb Chops Baked in Parchment

Serves 4
Working time: about 45 minutes
Total time: about 1 hour

Calories **245**
Protein **26g.**
Cholesterol **81mg.**
Total fat **9g.**
Saturated fat **4g.**
Sodium **205mg.**

8 lamb loin chops (about 2 lbs.), trimmed of fat
2 navel oranges
1 small cucumber, peeled and thinly sliced
2 tbsp. finely chopped red onion
¼ tsp. salt
freshly ground black pepper
2 tbsp. orange-flavored liqueur or orange juice
1 tsp. unsalted butter

Using a paring knife, cut all the peel and pith from the oranges. Slice each orange crosswise into 4 rounds; set the rounds aside.

Heat a large, nonstick skillet over medium-high heat; when the skillet is very hot, add the lamb chops and sear them for one minute on each side. Remove the chops from the skillet and set them aside.

Preheat the oven to 425° F. Cut four pieces of parchment paper or aluminum foil 16 inches by 24 inches. Fold each piece in half lengthwise, then cut each piece into a half-heart shape, as you would a valentine. Unfold and flatten out each heart.

Divide the orange rounds among the hearts, laying the rounds to one side of the center line so that only their edges touch it. Arrange the cucumber slices atop the oranges; sprinkle the onion, salt and some pepper over the cucumber. Lay two lamb chops on each portion, sprinkle them with the liqueur or orange juice, then lightly butter the uncovered half of the heart, leaving a 1-inch unbuttered border along the edge.

Fold the buttered half of the heart over the layered assembly and bring the edges together. Seal the package by crimping the edges together in a series of small, neat, overlapping folds.

Transfer the packages to a baking sheet; bake them for eight minutes for medium-rare lamb. Place the packages on individual plates and let each diner open his own at the table.

SUGGESTED ACCOMPANIMENT: *fennel sautéed with garlic.*

Roast Leg of Lamb with Pear Mustard

Serves 10
Working time: about 1 hour
Total time: about 2 hours and 15 minutes

Calories **225**
Protein **24g.**
Cholesterol **75mg.**
Total fat **9g.**
Saturated fat **3g.**
Sodium **430mg.**

one 5-lb. leg of lamb, trimmed of fat, the pelvic and thigh bones removed, the shank bone left in place (technique, page 105)
½ tbsp. Dijon mustard
1 tbsp. safflower oil
¼ tsp. salt
3 bunches scallions, trimmed and cut into 1-inch lengths

Pear mustard

½ tbsp. safflower oil
1½ lb. pears (preferably Comice), peeled, cored and coarsely chopped
1 cup unsalted brown stock or unsalted chicken stock (recipes, page 137)
1½ tbsp. fresh lemon juice
1 shallot, finely chopped, or 1 scallion, white part only, finely chopped
1 garlic clove, finely chopped
1¼ tsp. salt
freshly ground black pepper
1½ tbsp. Dijon mustard

To make the pear mustard, heat the oil in a heavy-bottomed saucepan set over medium-high heat. Add the pears and cook them, stirring frequently, until the juice is syrupy and lightly browned — 15 to 20 minutes. Add the stock, lemon juice, shallot or scallion, garlic, salt, some pepper and the mustard. Reduce the heat to medium and simmer the mixture, stirring occasionally, until only about 1½ cups remain — 15 to 20 minutes. Transfer the pear mustard to a food processor or a blender and purée it.

Preheat the oven to 325° F.

While the pear mustard is cooking, prepare the leg of lamb for roasting. Rub the ½ tablespoon of mustard over the exposed inner surface of the leg. Fold the meat over to enclose the mustard, then tie the leg securely with butcher's twine.

Heat the tablespoon of oil in a large, ovenproof skillet set over high heat. When the oil is hot, add the leg of lamb and brown it evenly on all sides — about 10 minutes. Sprinkle the lamb with the salt and transfer the skillet to the oven. Roast the lamb for 20 minutes, then coat it with about one third of the pear mustard and roast it for 20 minutes more. Brush the lamb with about half of the remaining pear mustard. Increase the oven temperature to 500° F. and cook the lamb until the pear mustard is lightly browned in places — 15 to 20 minutes. Remove the leg of lamb from the oven and let it rest for 20 minutes.

Blanch the scallion pieces in boiling water for one minute, then drain them and divide them among 10 warmed dinner plates. Slice the lamb and arrange the pieces on the scallions; dab a little of the remaining pear mustard on top before serving.

SUGGESTED ACCOMPANIMENT: *a gratin of sliced turnips and sweet potatoes.*

Mediterranean Lamb Salad

Serves 4
Working time: about 35 minutes
Total time: about 2 hours and 15 minutes

Calories **280**
Protein **32g.**
Cholesterol **96mg.**
Total fat **13g.**
Saturated fat **5g.**
Sodium **350mg.**

4 lamb shanks (about 3 lbs.), trimmed of fat
¼ tsp. salt
freshly ground black pepper
1 tbsp. olive oil
1 large onion (about ½ lb.), thinly sliced
2 garlic cloves, finely chopped
2 tsp. fresh thyme, or ½ tsp. dried thyme leaves
¾ tsp. dry mustard
⅓ cup cider vinegar
1 head of escarole (about 1 lb.), trimmed, washed, dried and cut crosswise into 1-inch-wide strips
1 large ripe tomato, cored and cut into thin wedges
1½ oz. feta cheese

Preheat the oven to 350° F. Sprinkle the lamb shanks with the salt and a generous grinding of pepper. Place the shanks in a heavy-bottomed roasting pan and bake them until they are tender — one hour and 30 minutes to two hours — turning them once after one hour and adding ¼ cup of water to the pan if the juices begin to burn. Remove the lamb from the oven and set it aside to cool; do not wash the roasting pan.

When the meat is cool enough to handle, pull it off the bones and tear it into shreds with your fingers. Transfer the meat to a bowl, cover it loosely with aluminum foil, and keep it warm.

Spoon off any fat that has accumulated in the roasting pan and set the pan over medium-low heat. Stir in the oil, onion, garlic, thyme, mustard and a generous grinding of pepper. Cook the mixture, scraping up the caramelized juices with a wooden spoon, until the onion is translucent — 10 to 15 minutes. Pour in the vinegar and continue cooking the mixture, stirring constantly, for one minute. Add the escarole and the tomato wedges, and keep stirring the salad until the escarole begins to wilt — about one minute. Stir in the shredded lamb and toss well.

Transfer the salad to a serving bowl. Crumble the cheese on top and serve the salad while it is still warm.

SUGGESTED ACCOMPANIMENT: *Italian bread.*

Lamb Loin Roast on a Bed of Spring Greens

ASK YOUR BUTCHER TO SAW THROUGH THE CHINE BONE
OF THE ROASTS SO YOU CAN CARVE THE MEAT.

Serves 8
Working time: about 40 minutes
Total time: about 1 hour and 30 minutes

Calories **225**
Protein **24g.**
Cholesterol **68mg.**
Total fat **11g.**
Saturated fat **3g.**
Sodium **195mg.**

2 lamb loin roasts (about 2½ lb. each), trimmed of fat
1 tbsp. olive oil
1 tbsp. grainy mustard
⅛ tsp. salt
freshly ground black pepper
2 garlic cloves, finely chopped
½ cup fresh whole-wheat bread crumbs
1 tbsp. chopped fresh parsley
1 tsp. chopped fresh thyme, or ¼ tsp. dried thyme leaves
1 tsp. chopped fresh rosemary, or ¼ tsp. dried rosemary, crumbled

Wilted spring-greens salad
1 tbsp. olive oil
2 scallions, trimmed and chopped
1 lb. dandelion greens, mustard greens or spinach, stemmed, washed and dried
1 bunch watercress, trimmed, washed and dried
16 cherry tomatoes, cut in half
1 tbsp. red wine vinegar
⅛ tsp. salt
freshly ground black pepper

Set the lamb roasts in a roasting pan with their bone sides down. In a small bowl, combine 1 teaspoon of the oil, the mustard, salt, some pepper and half of the garlic. Rub this mixture over the lamb and let it stand at room temperature for one hour.

Preheat the oven to 450° F. Roast the lamb until it has browned — about 15 minutes. In the meantime, mix together the bread crumbs, parsley, thyme, rosemary, the remaining garlic and some pepper.

Sprinkle the bread-crumb mixture over the top of the lamb roasts; dribble the remaining 2 teaspoons of oil over the bread crumbs. Continue roasting the lamb until the bread crumbs have browned and the meat is medium rare — about 10 minutes more, or until a meat thermometer inserted in the center registers 140° F. Keep the lamb warm while you make the salad.

For the salad, heat the tablespoon of olive oil in a skillet over medium-high heat. Add the scallions and sauté them for 45 seconds. Add the greens or spinach, along with the watercress, tomatoes and vinegar. Toss the vegetables in the skillet until the greens are slightly wilted — about 30 seconds. Remove the pan from the heat and season the salad with the salt and some pepper.

Carve the lamb roasts into 16 pieces and serve them atop the salad.

SUGGESTED ACCOMPANIMENTS: *steamed new potatoes; cloverleaf rolls.*

Roast Leg of Lamb with Nectarine Chutney

Serves 10
Working time: about 1 hour and 15 minutes
Total time: about 2 hours

Calories **285**
Protein **25g.**
Cholesterol **75mg.**
Total fat **8g.**
Saturated fat **3g.**
Sodium **215mg.**

one 5-lb. leg of lamb, trimmed of fat
5 garlic cloves, finely chopped
2 tbsp. chopped fresh rosemary, or 1 tbsp. dried rosemary, crumbled
½ cup Dijon mustard
freshly ground black pepper
Nectarine chutney
¾ cup cider vinegar
¼ cup light brown sugar
4 shallots, finely chopped, or 1 small onion, finely chopped
1 garlic clove, finely chopped
¼ cup golden raisins
¼ cup dark raisins
1 tbsp. finely chopped crystallized ginger, or 2 tsp. finely chopped fresh ginger
¼ tsp. hot red-pepper flakes
¼ tsp. ground cinnamon
2½ lb. nectarines, pitted and cut into ½-inch cubes
1½ tbsp. chopped fresh parsley

Preheat the oven to 475° F.

To make the chutney, combine the vinegar and brown sugar in a heavy-bottomed, nonreactive saucepan set over medium-high heat; bring the mixture to a boil, then reduce the heat, and simmer the mixture for two minutes. Stir in the shallots, garlic, raisins, ginger, red-pepper flakes, cinnamon and nectarines, and cook the chutney until the liquid has reduced by half — about 20 minutes. Mix in the parsley and set the chutney aside to cool to room temperature.

While the chutney is cooking, put the lamb into a roasting pan and roast it until it has browned — about 15 minutes. In a small bowl, combine the garlic, rosemary, mustard and some pepper. Brush the top of the leg of lamb with this mixture.

Return the lamb to the oven and roast it for 20 minutes more. Reduce the heat to 350° F. and roast the lamb for another 30 minutes for medium-rare meat, or until a meat thermometer inserted in the center registers 140° F.

Remove the lamb from the oven and let it rest for 20 minutes. Carve the lamb and serve the slices with the chutney alongside.

SUGGESTED ACCOMPANIMENTS: *roasted potatoes; steamed carrot sticks.*

Leg of Lamb Stuffed with Vegetables

Serves 10
Working time: about 40 minutes
Total time: about 2 hours

Calories **240**
Protein **25g.**
Cholesterol **77mg.**
Total fat **11g.**
Saturated fat **4g.**
Sodium **235mg.**

one 5-lb. leg of lamb, trimmed of fat and boned (technique, page 105)
2 tbsp. safflower oil
1 large carrot, julienned
1 large zucchini, julienned
1 large yellow squash, julienned
½ cup dry sherry
⅓ cup freshly grated Parmesan cheese (about 1 oz.)
½ tsp. salt
freshly ground black pepper
1 tbsp. fresh thyme, or 2 tsp. dried thyme leaves
1 cup unsalted brown stock or unsalted chicken stock (recipes, page 137)
2 tbsp. finely chopped shallot or onion
1½ tbsp. cornstarch, mixed with 2 tbsp. water

To prepare the stuffing, heat 1 tablespoon of the oil in a large, ovenproof skillet over medium heat. Add the carrot julienne and sauté it, stirring often, for two minutes. Stir in the zucchini and yellow squash, and cook the vegetables until the carrot is barely tender — about two minutes more. Remove the skillet from the heat

and pour in 2 tablespoons of the sherry. Add the Parmesan cheese and toss the stuffing to mix it well.

Preheat the oven to 325° F. Spread out the boned leg of lamb on a work surface and season it with ¼ teaspoon of the salt, some pepper and half of the thyme. Spread the stuffing over the leg of lamb and roll it up as you would a jelly roll. Tie the leg of lamb with butcher's twine to secure it.

Wipe out the skillet and heat the remaining tablespoon of oil in it over high heat. Add the lamb roll and brown it on all sides — two to three minutes altogether. Put the skillet into the oven and roast the lamb until it is tender — about one hour. Transfer the roast to a platter and set it aside.

Discard the fat and set the skillet on the stove top over low heat. Add the stock, the remaining thyme, the shallot or onion, and the remaining sherry to the skillet, then scrape the bottom with a wooden spoon to dissolve the caramelized roasting juices. Increase the heat to medium high and boil the liquid until about one third of it remains — seven to 10 minutes. Reduce the heat to low and whisk in the cornstarch mixture. Cook the sauce, stirring continuously, until it has thickened — about one minute. Season the sauce with the remaining ¼ teaspoon of salt and some pepper.

Cut the roast into slices. Pour the sauce into a sauceboat and pass it separately.

SUGGESTED ACCOMPANIMENTS: *broccoli; mashed potatoes.*

Lamb Noisettes on Zucchini Pancakes

NOISETTES ARE SMALL, ROUND SLICES
CUT FROM THE BONED LOIN.

Serves 4
Working (and total) time: about 30 minutes

Calories **235**
Protein **26g.**
Cholesterol **71mg.**
Total fat **9g.**
Saturated fat **4g.**
Sodium **295mg.**

one 2½-lb. lamb loin roast, trimmed of fat and boned (technique, page 89)
3 tbsp. cut chives or finely chopped scallions for garnish
Zucchini pancakes
2 zucchini (about ¾ lb.), grated
1 carrot, grated
1 egg white
3 tbsp. freshly grated Parmesan cheese
2 tbsp. whole-wheat flour
2 garlic cloves, finely chopped
¼ tsp. salt
freshly ground black pepper
1 tsp. safflower oil

Cut the lamb loin into eight slices. With a meat mallet or the flat of a heavy knife, pound each slice between heavy-duty plastic wrap or wax paper to a thickness of about ¼ inch. Set the noisettes aside.

Combine all the pancake ingredients but the oil in a bowl and mix them well.

Heat a large, nonstick skillet over medium heat. Add the oil and spread it over the bottom with a paper towel. Drop four 2-tablespoon mounds of the pancake mixture into the skillet, allowing ample room between them. With a spatula, spread out each mound to form a pancake about 3 inches in diameter. Cook the pancakes until they are lightly browned — about three minutes per side. Transfer the pancakes to a cookie sheet and keep them warm. Cook four more pancakes the same way.

Increase the heat under the skillet to high. Add the noisettes to the skillet and cook them until they are browned — about two minutes per side.

Put two zucchini pancakes on each of four plates; top each pancake with a noisette. Sprinkle the noisettes with the chives or scallions, and serve at once.

SUGGESTED ACCOMPANIMENT: *tomato wedges with basil.*

Stir-Fried Lamb
with Green Beans

Serves 4
Working (and total) time: about 30 minutes

Calories **245**
Protein **25g.**
Cholesterol **75mg.**
Total fat **12g.**
Saturated fat **3g.**
Sodium **325mg.**

1¼ lb. lean lamb (from the leg or loin), trimmed of fat and cut into thin strips
1 cup unsalted brown stock or unsalted chicken stock (recipes, page 137)
2 tbsp. brandy
2 tsp. low-sodium soy sauce
1½ tbsp. rice vinegar
1 shallot, chopped
¼ tsp. salt
½ lb. green beans, trimmed and cut in half on the diagonal
1½ tbsp. safflower oil
3 or 4 small dried red chili peppers, finely chopped (caution, page 23), or 1 tsp. hot red-pepper flakes
2 tsp. finely chopped fresh ginger
4 garlic cloves, finely chopped

Heat the stock in a small saucepan set over medium heat. Add the brandy, soy sauce, vinegar, shallot and salt, and simmer the mixture until it is reduced to about ¼ cup — 15 to 20 minutes. Set the sauce aside.

While the sauce is simmering, pour enough water into a saucepan to fill it about 1 inch deep. Set a vegetable steamer in the pan and bring the water to a boil. Put the beans into the steamer, cover the pan tightly, and steam the beans until they are tender but still crisp — about three minutes. Remove the beans from the pan and refresh them under cold running water. Set the beans aside.

Heat the oil in a large, nonstick skillet or a well-seasoned wok over high heat. Add the chili peppers or pepper flakes, the ginger and the garlic, and stir fry them for one minute. Add the beans and lamb, and continue stir frying until the meat is lightly browned and just cooked through — about two minutes. Pour the sauce over the lamb and beans, stir well, and cook the mixture for 30 seconds more. Serve immediately.

SUGGESTED ACCOMPANIMENT: *rice noodles.*

Kasha-Coated Lamb with Parsley-Garlic Sauce

Serves 4

Working (and total) time: about 20 minutes

Calories **315**
Protein **29g.**
Cholesterol **82mg.**
Total fat **13g.**
Saturated fat **4g.**
Sodium **220mg.**

4 lamb slices (about ¼ lb. each), cut from the sirloin end of the leg
1 egg white
1 tbsp. fresh lemon juice
1 cup kasha (toasted buckwheat groats)
¼ tsp. salt
freshly ground black pepper
1 tbsp. olive oil
½ tbsp. unsalted butter
1 shallot, finely chopped
1 garlic clove, finely chopped
1 cup chopped fresh parsley
1 ripe tomato, peeled, seeded and puréed in a food processor or a blender

Place one of the lamb slices between two sheets of plastic wrap or wax paper, and pound it with a meat mallet or the flat of a heavy knife until it is about ¼ inch thick. Flatten the other slices the same way.

In a shallow bowl, whisk together the egg white and lemon juice. Spread the kasha on a plate. Sprinkle the lamb slices with the salt and some pepper. Dip a slice in the egg-white mixture, then dredge it in the kasha, coating both sides. Repeat the process to coat the remaining slices of lamb.

Heat the oil and butter in a large, nonstick skillet over high heat. Add the coated lamb slices and cook them until they are lightly browned on one side — about three minutes. Turn the slices and cook them for two minutes more to brown the second side. Transfer the slices to a warmed platter.

Add the shallot, garlic and parsley to the skillet and cook them for one minute. Stir in the tomato purée and a generous grinding of black pepper. Cook the mixture for one minute more, then pour it over the lamb. Serve immediately.

SUGGESTED ACCOMPANIMENTS: *egg noodles; carrot purée.*

Lamb with Eggplant and Parmesan

Serves 4
Working (and total) time: about 1 hour and 15 minutes

Calories **450**
Protein **34g.**
Cholesterol **78mg.**
Total fat **10g.**
Saturated fat **4g.**
Sodium **235mg.**

1 lb. lean lamb (from the leg or loin), cut into ½-inch pieces
½ lb. pasta shells
1 tsp. olive oil
½ lb. pearl onions, blanched in boiling water for 2 minutes and peeled
½ lb. small mushrooms, wiped clean
¾ lb. eggplant, cut into ½-inch cubes
1 tsp. fresh thyme, or ½ tsp. dried thyme leaves
freshly ground black pepper
½ oz. Parmesan cheese, shaved with a vegetable peeler or grated (about ¼ cup)

Add the pasta to 3 quarts of boiling water with 1½ teaspoons of salt. Start testing the pasta for doneness after six minutes and cook it until it is *al dente*. Drain the pasta, rinse it under cold running water to prevent the shells from sticking together, and set it aside.

Heat a large, nonstick skillet over high heat. Add the pieces of lamb and sauté them until they are browned on all sides — about three minutes. Reduce the heat to medium and cook the lamb for three minutes more. Remove the lamb from the skillet and set the meat aside.

Add the olive oil and onions to the skillet. Place the cover on the skillet and cook the onions, stirring occasionally, until they are browned — about 15 minutes. Add the mushrooms and eggplant, then increase the heat to high, and sauté the vegetables until all are browned and the mushrooms and eggplant are soft — six to eight minutes.

Return the lamb to the skillet; add the pasta, the thyme and a generous grinding of pepper. Sauté the mixture until the pasta is heated through — about three minutes. Spoon the mixture into a serving dish and top it with the cheese. Serve immediately.

SUGGESTED ACCOMPANIMENT: *curly endive salad.*

Lamb and Barley Salad

Serves 4
Working time: about 20 minutes
Total time: about 2 hours (includes chilling)

Calories **255** Protein **17g.** Cholesterol **46mg.** Total fat **10g.** Saturated fat **2g.** Sodium **180mg.**	¾ lb. lean lamb (from the leg or loin), trimmed of fat and cut into ½-inch cubes
	½ cup pearl barley
	1½ tbsp. finely chopped fresh oregano, or ½ tbsp. dried oregano
	1½ tbsp. olive oil
	¼ tsp. salt
	freshly ground black pepper
	3 tbsp. red wine vinegar
	1 ripe tomato, seeded and chopped
	1 celery stalk, chopped
	½ cup chopped red onion
	several leaves of Boston lettuce, washed and dried, for garnish

Put the barley, half of the oregano and 3 cups of water into a saucepan. Bring the water to a boil, then reduce the heat to maintain a steady simmer. Cover the pan and cook the barley until it is tender — about 50 minutes. Drain the barley, transfer it to a bowl, and stir in ½ tablespoon of the oil.

Heat the remaining tablespoon of oil in a heavy-bottomed skillet set over high heat. Add the lamb cubes and sprinkle them with the salt and some pepper. Sauté the lamb, stirring frequently, until it is lightly browned — about two minutes. Pour in the vinegar and cook the mixture for 30 seconds longer.

Transfer the contents of the skillet to the bowl with the barley. Add the tomato, celery, onion, the remaining oregano and a generous grinding of pepper. Toss the salad well and chill it for at least one hour.

Just before serving, arrange the lettuce leaves on a plate or platter and mound the salad on top.

SUGGESTED ACCOMPANIMENT: *melon slices.*

Braised Leg of Lamb with White Beans

Serves 12
Working time: about 1 hour
Total time: about 3 hours and 30 minutes

Calories **310**
Protein **30g.**
Cholesterol **67mg.**
Total fat **8g.**
Saturated fat **3g.**
Sodium **455mg.**

one 5-lb. leg of lamb, trimmed of fat and boned (technique, page 105), the bones reserved
½ cup parsley leaves
8 garlic cloves
2 tbsp. fresh thyme, or 1 tbsp. dried thyme leaves
zest of three lemons
2 tsp. salt
freshly ground black pepper
1 tbsp. safflower oil
2½ cups dried navy beans, picked over and rinsed
1 cup dry white wine
4 cups unsalted chicken stock (recipe, page 137)
42 oz. canned unsalted whole tomatoes, crushed in their juice
1 lb. pearl onions, blanched for 2 minutes in boiling water and peeled

Place the parsley, garlic, thyme and lemon zest on a cutting board and finely chop them all together. Spread the lamb flat, with the boned side up, and rub the herbs and zest into the exposed surface. Season the lamb with 1 teaspoon of the salt and a generous grinding of pepper. Roll up the meat; tie it with butcher's twine *(technique, page 25)*.

Heat the oil in a large, heavy-bottomed, nonreactive pot or Dutch oven over high heat. Add the lamb and brown it on all sides — about three minutes per side. Reduce the heat to low and add the bones, beans, wine, stock, tomatoes and the remaining 1 teaspoon

of salt. Cover the pot, with the lid slightly ajar, and simmer the lamb for three hours.

Stir the pearl onions into the lamb and beans and cook the mixture for 30 minutes more. When the lamb is done, remove and discard the bones and transfer the meat to a cutting board. Skim off any fat that may have accumulated on the surface of the liquid. Discard the string and carve the lamb into 16 slices. Serve the slices on a platter surrounded by the beans, with the braising liquid poured over all.

SUGGESTED ACCOMPANIMENT: *steamed spinach.*

Boning a Leg of Lamb

1 REMOVING THE EXCESS FAT. Place a leg of lamb flat on the work surface. With a boning knife, trim away the fat, removing it in strips. Continue to cut around the leg until the entire fatty layer is removed; discard the trimmings.

2 LOOSENING THE PELVIC BONE. Cut around the edges of the pelvic bone at the thick end of the leg. Following the bone's contours and tilting the blade toward the bone, use short strokes to free it (below). Sever the bone by inserting the knife tip into the socket.

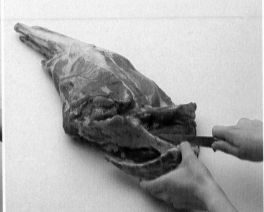
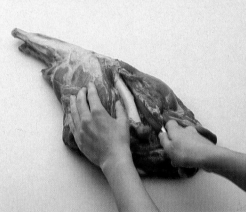
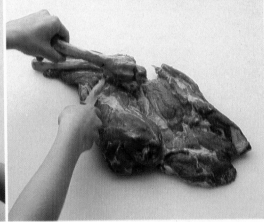

3 EXPOSING THE LEG BONE. Turn the leg so that the less meaty side faces up. Slice along the length of the leg bone to expose it. Work around the bone with short cutting strokes (above) to loosen it; the bone will still be attached to the smaller hind shank bone. Gently turn back the meat as you go.

4 REMOVING THE BONES. Slice along the length of the hind shank bone to expose it, and cut around it to detach it from the surrounding flesh. Lift the leg bone (above) so that it will be easier for you to get at the hind shank, and continue to cut until both bones come free. Discard all the bones.

Lamb Shanks with Orange and Cinnamon

Serves 4
Working time: about 45 minutes
Total time: about 3 hours

Calories **285**
Protein **20g.**
Cholesterol **52mg.**
Total fat **10g.**
Saturated fat **2g.**
Sodium **255mg.**

4 lamb shanks (about ¾ lb. each), trimmed of fat
⅓ cup flour
freshly ground black pepper
2 tbsp. chopped fresh oregano, or 2 tsp. dried oregano
1½ tbsp. safflower oil
1 onion, chopped
2 garlic cloves, finely chopped
½ cup red wine
¼ cup fresh orange juice
¼ tsp. salt
1 bay leaf
1 cinnamon stick, or ¼ tsp. ground cinnamon
2 cups pearl onions (about 10 oz.), blanched for 2 minutes in boiling water and peeled
1 lb. carrots, cut crosswise into 2-inch-long pieces
1 tbsp. julienned orange zest
¼ cup finely chopped parsley

Put the flour, some pepper and half of the oregano into a large plastic bag. Add the shanks and shake the bag to coat the meat with the mixture.

Heat the oil in a large heavy-bottomed skillet over medium-high heat. Sauté the shanks in the skillet, turning them from time to time, until they have browned. Add the chopped onion, reduce the heat to low, and cover the skillet. Cook the lamb and onion for five minutes, stirring occasionally.

Increase the heat to medium-high and add the garlic, wine, orange juice and 3 cups of water. Bring the liquid to a simmer, scraping the bottom of the skillet with a wooden spoon to dissolve any caramelized juices. Add the salt, bay leaf, cinnamon and the remaining oregano. Reduce the heat, cover the skillet, and continue simmering the meat until it is barely tender — one and a half to two hours.

Skim any fat from the surface of the liquid; add the pearl onions, carrots and orange zest. Simmer the lamb, partially covered, until the vegetables are tender — about 30 minutes.

Skim off any more fat, stir in the chopped parsley, and serve the lamb with the vegetables and the sauce.

SUGGESTED ACCOMPANIMENT: *yellow rice.*

Lamb Meatballs with Lentils

Serves 6
Working time: about 45 minutes
Total time: about 1 hour and 30 minutes

Calories **280**
Protein **25g.**
Cholesterol **52mg.**
Total fat **8g.**
Saturated fat **3g.**
Sodium **205mg.**

1¼ lb. lean lamb (from the leg or loin), trimmed of fat and ground (box, page 8)
¼ cup dry bread crumbs
2 tbsp. freshly grated Parmesan cheese
1 tbsp. chopped fresh rosemary, or 1 tsp. dried rosemary, crumbled
2 tsp. olive oil
1 turnip, chopped
1 onion, chopped
2 carrots, chopped
2 celery stalks, chopped
½ lb. fresh mushrooms, wiped clean and thinly sliced
4 garlic cloves, finely chopped
½ tsp. hot red-pepper flakes
1 cup lentils, picked over
⅛ tsp. salt
3 cups unsalted chicken stock (recipe, page 137)

Mix together the lamb, bread crumbs, cheese and rosemary. With your hands, form the mixture into 12 balls. Heat the oil in a large, nonstick or heavy-bottomed skillet set over high heat. Add the meatballs and brown them all over — four to five minutes. Remove the meatballs from the skillet with a slotted spoon and set them aside.

Add the turnip, onion, carrots, celery, mushrooms, garlic and red-pepper flakes to the skillet. Reduce the heat to low and sauté the vegetables until they are soft — about eight minutes.

Increase the heat to medium high. Add the lentils, salt and stock, and bring the liquid to a boil. Add the meatballs, cover the skillet with the lid ajar, and reduce the heat to low. Simmer the meatballs and lentils until the lentils are tender — about 45 minutes.

Serve the meatballs and lentils piping hot.

SUGGESTED ACCOMPANIMENT: *carrot and zucchini salad.*

Loin Chops with Lima Beans

Serves 4
Working time: about 15 minutes
Total time: about 30 minutes

Calories **340**
Protein **32g.**
Cholesterol **77mg.**
Total fat **11g.**
Saturated fat **4g.**
Sodium **255mg.**

4 lamb loin chops (about 5 oz. each), trimmed of fat
freshly ground black pepper
2 tsp. safflower oil
1 paper-thin slice of prosciutto or other dry-cured ham (about 1 oz.), cut into thin strips
1 onion, finely chopped
2 garlic cloves, finely chopped
14 oz. canned unsalted whole tomatoes, seeded and coarsely chopped, with their juice
2 tbsp. chopped fresh basil, or 2 tsp. dried basil
1 tsp. red wine vinegar
2 cups lima beans
⅛ tsp. salt

Season the loin chops with pepper. Heat the oil in a heavy-bottomed skillet set over medium-high heat. Add the chops and sear them on both sides — about one minute per side. Transfer the chops to a plate. Add the prosciutto and onion to the skillet, reduce the heat to medium, and cook the mixture, stirring frequently, until the onions have become translucent — about four minutes. Add the garlic and cook the mixture for one minute more.

Return the chops to the skillet and then add the tomatoes and their juice, the basil, vinegar, lima beans and salt; bring the mixture to a simmer. Partially cover the skillet, reduce the heat to low, and simmer the mixture until the chops are firm yet slightly springy to the touch — about 10 minutes. Serve the lamb and vegetables at once.

SUGGESTED ACCOMPANIMENT: *orzo tossed with chives.*

Braised Leg of Lamb with Mustard Seeds

Serves 8
Working time: about 40 minutes
Total time: about 3 hours and 15 minutes

Calories **205**	
Protein **20g.**	one 3-lb. leg of lamb, shank half, trimmed of fat
Cholesterol **56mg.**	1 tbsp. olive oil
Total fat **7g.**	12 oz. dark beer
Saturated fat **2g.**	1 cup unsalted brown stock (recipe, page 137)
Sodium **155**	2 onions, quartered
	3 garlic cloves
	1 tsp. mustard seeds
	½ tsp. celery seeds
	¼ tsp. salt
	freshly ground black pepper
	4 bay leaves
	3 whole cloves
	1 small rutabaga (about 1 lb.), peeled and cut into 1-inch cubes
	1 small green cabbage (about 2 lb.), quartered and cored, the leaves separated

Heat the oil in a large, heavy-bottomed casserole set over high heat. When the oil is hot, add the lamb and brown it on all sides — about 10 minutes in all. Pour in the beer and the stock, then add the onions, garlic, mustard seeds, celery seeds, salt and some pepper. Tie up the bay leaves and cloves in a piece of cheesecloth, and add them to the casserole. Bring the liquid to a boil, then reduce the heat to maintain a simmer.

Partly cover the casserole and braise the lamb for about one hour and 15 minutes, turning it two or three times during the cooking. Add the rutabaga cubes and continue braising the lamb until it is tender — approximately 30 minutes more.

While the rutabagas are cooking, pour enough water into a large pot to fill it about 1 inch deep. Set a vegetable steamer in the pot, add the cabbage, and cover the pot. Bring the water to a boil and steam the cabbage until it is tender — about 20 minutes.

Transfer the cabbage to a large platter and cover it loosely with aluminum foil. Remove the lamb from the casserole and set it on a cutting board. With a slotted spoon, transfer the rutabaga and onions to a bowl and cover them with foil too.

Remove the bundle of bay leaves and cloves from the casserole and discard it. Reduce the sauce over high heat until only about 1 cup of it remains — about 10 minutes. Carve the lamb and arrange the slices on the cabbage. Surround the lamb with the rutabaga and onions, then pour the sauce over all. Serve at once.

SUGGESTED ACCOMPANIMENT: *whole-wheat bread.*

Mexican Lamb

IN THIS DISH, LAMB IS PAIRED WITH A VERSION
OF THE MEXICAN MOLE POBLANO, A SPICY CONCOCTION
FEATURING CHILI PEPPERS AND CHOCOLATE.

Serves 8
Working time: about 45 minutes
Total time: about 1 hour and 45 minutes

Calories **220**
Protein **24g.**
Cholesterol **75mg.**
Total fat **11g.**
Saturated fat **3g.**
Sodium **210mg.**

2½ lb. lean lamb (from the leg or loin), trimmed of fat and cut into ½-inch cubes
2 tbsp. olive oil
5 garlic cloves, finely chopped
1 jalapeño pepper, seeded, deribbed and finely chopped (caution, page 23)
1 tsp. cumin seeds
1 onion, cut into ½-inch cubes
1 green pepper, seeded, deribbed and cut into ½-inch pieces
2 large ripe tomatoes, peeled, seeded and cut into ½-inch pieces
1 cup unsalted brown stock or unsalted chicken stock (recipes, page 137)
½ tsp. salt
¼ tsp. grated nutmeg
1½ tbsp. unsweetened cocoa powder

Heat 1 tablespoon of the olive oil in a large, heavy-bottomed skillet set over high heat. Add half of the lamb cubes and sauté them until they are browned on all sides — five to seven minutes. With a slotted spoon, remove the cubes from the skillet and transfer them to a bowl. Return the skillet to the heat; pour in ½ tablespoon of the remaining oil, and brown the rest of the lamb cubes. Set them aside also.

Add the remaining ½ tablespoon of oil to the skillet and return it to the heat. Add the garlic, jalapeño pepper and cumin seeds, and cook the mixture until the garlic is lightly browned — about one minute. Add the onion, green pepper, tomatoes, stock, salt and nutmeg, and bring the mixture to a simmer. Return the lamb cubes and their juices to the skillet, then stir in the cocoa powder. Reduce the heat to low and simmer the stew, stirring occasionally, until the meat is very tender and the sauce has thickened — about one hour. Remove the stew from the heat and let it stand for 10 minutes before serving.

SUGGESTED ACCOMPANIMENT: *corn tortillas.*

Lamb Shanks with Chick-Peas

Serves 6
Working time: about 30 minutes
Total time: about 2 hours and 30 minutes

Calories **240**
Protein **25g.**
Cholesterol **52mg.**
Total fat **6g.**
Saturated fat **2g.**
Sodium **185mg.**

4 lamb shanks (about 3 lbs.), trimmed of fat
½ lb. dried chick-peas, picked over
2 cups unsalted brown stock or unsalted chicken stock (recipes, page 137)
¼ tsp. salt
freshly ground black pepper
¾ tsp. ground coriander
1 onion, quartered
3 garlic cloves, thinly sliced
1 tbsp. tomato paste
1½ tsp. fresh thyme, or ½ tsp. dried thyme leaves
1 tbsp. fresh lemon juice

Rinse the chick-peas under cold running water, then put them into a large, heavy-bottomed pot, and pour in enough water to cover them by about 3 inches. Cover the pot, leaving the lid ajar, and slowly bring the liquid to a boil over medium-low heat. Boil the chick-peas for two minutes, then turn off the heat and soak them, covered, for at least one hour.

Place the lamb shanks in a large pot filled with 2 quarts of water. Bring the water to a boil and blanch the lamb for three minutes. Drain the lamb shanks, transfer them to a plate, and set the plate aside.

Drain the chick-peas and return them to the large, heavy-bottomed pot. Pour in 4 cups of water and the stock, and bring the liquid to a boil over high heat. Add the blanched lamb shanks and the salt, some pepper and the coriander. Reduce the heat to maintain a simmer and cook the lamb and chick-peas for 45 minutes.

Add the onion, garlic, tomato paste, thyme and lemon juice to the lamb and chick-peas, and stir to combine them. Simmer the mixture until the lamb is very tender — one hour to one hour and 30 minutes.

With a slotted spoon, remove the lamb shanks from the pot and transfer them to a plate. Let them stand until they are cool enough to handle. Skim the fat from the surface of the chick-pea mixture and keep the mixture warm. Remove the meat from the shank bones and cut it into ½-inch pieces; discard the bones. Return the lamb pieces to the pot.

This dish can be served immediately or prepared one day in advance. To reheat, add ½ cup of water to the mixture, bring it to a simmer over low heat, and cook it for 10 minutes.

SUGGESTED ACCOMPANIMENTS: *French bread; green salad.*

Red Pepper and Okra Lamb Stew

Serves 4
Working time: about 20 minutes
Total time: about 1 hour

Calories **355**
Protein **28g.**
Cholesterol **75mg.**
Total fat **11g.**
Saturated fat **3g.**
Sodium **190mg.**

1¼ lb. lean lamb (from the leg or loin), trimmed of fat and cut into 1-inch pieces
¼ cup flour
2 tbsp. paprika
⅛ tsp. salt
freshly ground black pepper
1 tbsp. safflower oil
1 onion, finely chopped
1½ cups unsalted brown stock or unsalted chicken stock (recipes, page 137)
2 tsp. cider vinegar
1 tsp. Dijon mustard
8 drops hot red-pepper sauce
1 garlic clove, finely chopped
1 sweet red pepper, seeded, deribbed and cut into 1-inch squares
½ lb. okra, trimmed, cut in half if large
½ cup rice

Combine the flour and paprika in a large bowl. Season the lamb pieces with the salt and some pepper, then toss them in the flour mixture. Remove the meat from the bowl, shaking off any excess flour, and set it aside.

Heat the oil in an ovenproof casserole over medium-high heat. Add the lamb and onion and cook them, stirring continuously, until the onion is translucent and the meat is browned — two to three minutes. Stir in the stock, vinegar, mustard, hot red-pepper sauce, garlic, sweet red pepper and okra, and bring the mixture to a simmer. Reduce the heat to low and simmer the stew, stirring every now and then, until the meat is tender — 30 to 40 minutes.

Meanwhile, bring 1 cup of water to a boil in a saucepan. Add the rice, tightly cover the pan, and reduce the heat to medium low. Cook the rice until all the liquid has been absorbed — about 20 minutes.

When the meat is tender, stir the cooked rice into the stew and serve at once.

SUGGESTED ACCOMPANIMENT: *mixed green salad.*

Lamb Poached in Buttermilk

Serves 4
Working time: about 15 minutes
Total time: about 1 hour and 15 minutes

Calories **480**
Protein **34g.**
Cholesterol **78mg.**
Total fat **13g.**
Saturated fat **3g.**
Sodium **410mg.**

1¼ lb. lean lamb (from the leg or loin), trimmed of fat and cut into ¾-inch cubes
2 tsp. safflower oil
1 green pepper, seeded, deribbed and cut into 1-inch squares
1 onion, cut into 1-inch cubes
¼ tsp. salt
⅛ tsp. white pepper
1 large carrot, cut into 1-inch pieces
2 tsp. caraway seeds
cayenne pepper
1½ cups unsalted chicken stock (recipe, page 137)
1 cup buttermilk
1½ tbsp. cornstarch
½ lb. dried egg noodles

Heat the oil in a large saucepan set over medium heat. Add the green pepper and onion and cook them, stirring frequently, until the onion is translucent — about five minutes. Add the lamb, salt, some white pepper, the carrot pieces, the caraway seeds, a pinch of cayenne pepper and the stock; bring the liquid to a simmer. Mix the buttermilk and cornstarch in a small bowl, then whisk them into the simmering liquid. Partly cover the saucepan and simmer the lamb until it is tender — about 45 minutes.

Add the noodles to 3 quarts of boiling water with 1½ teaspoons of salt. Start testing the noodles after six minutes and cook them until they are *al dente*. Drain the noodles and transfer them to a serving dish. Top the noodles with the lamb and serve at once.

SUGGESTED ACCOMPANIMENT: *zucchini cooked with shallots.*

Lamb-and-Eggplant Terrine

Serves 8
Working time: about 1 hour and 20 minutes
Total time: about 9 hours (includes chilling)

Calories **285**
Protein **31g.**
Cholesterol **94mg.**
Total fat **12g.**
Saturated fat **4g.**
Sodium **220mg.**

2½ lb. leg of lamb, sirloin half, trimmed of fat and boned (technique, page 105)
2 sweet red peppers
2 tbsp. olive oil
1 onion, chopped
3 garlic cloves, thinly sliced
½ tbsp. chopped fresh oregano, or ½ tsp. dried oregano
½ tbsp. fresh thyme, or ½ tsp. dried thyme leaves
½ tsp. salt
freshly ground black pepper
28 oz. canned unsalted whole tomatoes, drained, or 3 ripe tomatoes, peeled, seeded and chopped
2 tbsp. red wine vinegar
1 large eggplant (about 1¾ lb.)
½ tbsp. fresh lemon juice

Broil the peppers, turning them with tongs as they blister, until their skins are blackened all over — about 15 minutes. Transfer the peppers to a bowl and cover it with plastic wrap. When the peppers are cool enough to handle, peel, seed and coarsely chop them, reserving their juice.

Heat ½ tablespoon of the oil in a saucepan over medium-low heat. Add the onion, garlic, oregano, thyme, ¼ teaspoon of the salt and some black pepper. Cook the mixture, stirring occasionally, until the onion is translucent — about five minutes. Add the tomatoes, the peppers and their juice, and the vinegar. Simmer the sauce until it has thickened — about seven minutes. Purée the sauce in a food processor or a blender and return it to the pan.

With a small, sharp knife, remove four long strips of skin from the eggplant; each strip should be about ½ inch wide. Set the strips aside. Slice the eggplant itself into ¼-inch-thick slices; sprinkle the slices with the lemon juice and the remaining ¼ teaspoon of salt.

Broil the eggplant slices on a large, nonreactive baking sheet for five minutes. Set the eggplant slices aside until you are ready to assemble the terrine.

Cut the boned lamb into ¼-inch-thick slices. Place each slice between plastic wrap or wax paper; pound the slices with a meat mallet or the flat of a heavy knife to a thickness of about ⅛ inch.

Heat 1 tablespoon of the remaining oil in a large, nonstick skillet over high heat. Add one fourth of the lamb slices and sauté them for 30 seconds per side. Remove the slices and sauté a second batch; set the second batch aside. Pour the remaining ½ tablespoon of oil into the pan and sauté the remaining lamb slices in two final batches. After removing the last slices from the pan, pour in ¼ cup of water and stir to dislodge any caramelized juices; add this liquid to the tomato sauce.

Preheat the oven to 325° F. Lightly oil a 2-quart, nonreactive loaf pan. Arrange the strips of eggplant skin in a crisscross pattern in the bottom, their shiny sides down. Place a layer of eggplant slices on top, followed by some of the lamb slices and about ¼ cup of the sauce. Repeat the layering process until all the slices have been used, topping the terrine with a layer of eggplant. Reserve any remaining sauce.

Cover the top of the terrine with wax paper and set the terrine in the oven. To prevent the lamb slices from curling during cooking, weight the top of the terrine by placing another loaf pan filled partway with dried beans on top of the terrine.

Bake the terrine for 45 minutes. Remove the weight from the top and continue baking the terrine until the meat is tender — about 45 minutes more. Remove the terrine from the oven and allow it to stand at room temperature for 30 minutes. Chill the terrine for at least six hours.

To unmold the terrine, run a knife around the inside of the pan, then remove the wax paper and invert a platter over the top. Turn pan and platter over together. Wrap the terrine for a few seconds in a hot, wet dish towel, then carefully lift away the pan. Serve the terrine in slices, with any reserved sauce alongside.

SUGGESTED ACCOMPANIMENTS: *cucumber salad; pita bread.*

Lamb-and-Endive Gratin

Serves 4
Working time: about 45 minutes
Total time: about 1 hour and 30 minutes

Calories **335**
Protein **35g.**
Cholesterol **93mg.**
Total fat **16g.**
Saturated fat **7g.**
Sodium **337mg.**

one 2-lb. lamb loin roast, trimmed of fat and boned (technique, page 89)
1 tbsp. fresh lemon juice
4 heads of Belgian endive, trimmed
2 tsp. safflower oil
4 shallots, or 1 small onion, thinly sliced
1 tbsp. flour
¾ cup unsalted brown stock or unsalted chicken stock (recipes, page 137)
1 tbsp. Dijon mustard
freshly ground black pepper
½ cup dry bread crumbs
¼ lb. part-skim mozzarella, grated

Bring 1 quart of water to a boil in a large saucepan. Add the lemon juice and Belgian endive and cook them for five minutes. Drain the endive and rinse it under cold running water. When the endive is cool enough to handle, squeeze out the liquid with your hands. Quarter each endive lengthwise and set the pieces aside.

Preheat the oven to 400° F.

Slice the lamb into eight pieces. Place the slices between two pieces of plastic wrap or wax paper, and pound them with a meat mallet or the flat of a heavy knife until they are only about ¼ inch thick. Heat the oil in a large, nonstick skillet over high heat. Add the lamb slices and cook them for 30 seconds on each side. Remove the slices from the skillet and set them aside.

Reduce the heat to medium. Add the shallot or onion slices to the skillet; cook them, stirring continuous-ly, until they have browned — about five minutes. Remove the skillet from the heat and stir in the flour. Whisking constantly, pour in the stock in a slow, steady stream. Return the skillet to the heat and cook the sauce, stirring, until it thickens — about two minutes. Mix in the mustard and a generous grinding of pepper, then simmer the sauce for five minutes more.

Sprinkle 1 tablespoon of the bread crumbs into an 8-by-8-inch baking dish. Place the reserved lamb pieces on top of the crumbs and spread the endive quarters over the lamb. Pour the sauce over all; sprinkle the mozzarella and the remaining bread crumbs on top. Bake the gratin until the liquid bubbles and the top has browned — about 40 minutes.

SUGGESTED ACCOMPANIMENTS: *steamed asparagus; toasted French bread.*

Phyllo-Wrapped Lamb Medallions

A MEDALLION IS A SMALL OVAL OR ROUND SLICE OF MEAT.

Serves 4
Working time: about 25 minutes
Total time: about 45 minutes

Calories **325**
Protein **28g.**
Cholesterol **78mg.**
Total fat **12g.**
Saturated fat **4g.**
Sodium **320mg.**

one 2½-lb. lamb loin roast, trimmed of fat and boned (technique, page 89)
1 ripe pear
2 tsp. safflower oil
¼ tsp. salt
freshly ground black pepper
2 tsp. finely chopped fresh ginger
½ cup port or Madeira
1 tsp. red wine vinegar
½ cup unsalted brown stock or unsalted chicken stock (recipes, page 137)
4 sheets phyllo dough
1 egg white, lightly beaten
4 parsley sprigs (optional)

Peel the pear. (If you like, julienne some of the skin for a garnish and set it aside.) Halve and core the pear, then thinly slice one half, and set the slices aside. Chop the remaining half and set it aside, too.

Slice the lamb into four pieces. Place the pieces between two sheets of plastic wrap or wax paper; with a meat mallet or the flat of a heavy knife, pound the pieces to a thickness of about ½ inch. Heat the oil in a large, nonstick skillet over medium-high heat. Add the lamb medallions and sear them for one minute on each side. Remove the medallions from the skillet and season them with ⅛ teaspoon of the salt and some pepper; set the medallions aside.

Add the ginger, wine, vinegar and chopped pear to the skillet. Lower the heat and simmer the liquid until it is reduced by half — about seven minutes. Add the stock, the remaining salt and some pepper and return the liquid to a simmer. Transfer the sauce to a food processor or a blender, and purée it. Keep the sauce warm while you prepare the phyllo packages.

Preheat the oven to 425° F.

Fold one of the phyllo sheets in half. Pat a lamb medallion dry with a paper towel and position the medallion in the center of the folded phyllo sheet. Arrange one fourth of the pear slices on top, then fold the phyllo over the meat and fruit. Brush the seams with some of the beaten egg white. Put the phyllo package seam side down on a baking sheet. Brush the top with more egg white. Wrap the remaining lamb medallions and pear slices the same way.

Bake the packages for eight minutes for medium-rare lamb. Divide the sauce among four individual plates and set a phyllo package on each plate. Garnish each serving, if you like, with a sprig of parsley and some julienned pear skin.

SUGGESTED ACCOMPANIMENTS: *Brussels sprouts; rice.*

Lamb Chili Verde

Serves 6
Working time: about 30 minutes
Total time: about 2 hours and 30 minutes
(includes soaking)

Calories **310**
Protein **27g.**
Cholesterol **68mg.**
Total fat **10g.**
Saturated fat **4g.**
Sodium **210mg.**

1 ½ lb. lean lamb (from the leg or loin), trimmed of fat and cut into ½-inch pieces
1 cup dried pinto beans, picked over
1 tbsp. safflower oil
1 onion, finely chopped
¼ tsp. salt
freshly ground black pepper
2 garlic cloves, finely chopped
2 jalapeño peppers, seeded, deribbed and coarsely chopped (caution, page 23)
1 cucumber, peeled, seeded and coarsely chopped
1 ½ lb. green tomatoes, peeled, seeded and coarsely chopped, or 1 ½ lb. tomatillos, husks removed, stemmed, washed and quartered
1 ½ cups unsalted brown stock or unsalted chicken stock (recipes, page 137)
2 tbsp. dark brown sugar
½ tsp. cumin seeds
⅓ cup grated Cheddar cheese (about 1 oz.)

Rinse the pinto beans under cold running water, then put them into a large, heavy-bottomed pot, and pour in enough water to cover them by about 3 inches. Discard any beans that float to the surface. Cover the pot, leaving the lid ajar, and slowly bring the liquid to a boil over medium-low heat. Boil the beans for two minutes, then turn off the heat, and soak the beans, covered, for at least one hour. (Alternatively, soak the beans in cold water overnight.)

Heat the oil in a large, heavy-bottomed pot over medium-high heat. Add the lamb pieces and sauté them until they are browned on all sides — about three minutes. Reduce the heat to medium and add the onion, the salt and some pepper. Cook the mixture, stirring frequently, until the onion is translucent — about three minutes. Add the garlic and cook the mixture for one minute more. Drain the beans and add them to the pot. Stir in the jalapeño peppers, the cucumber, all but ½ cup of the tomatoes or tomatillos, the stock, brown sugar, cumin seeds and 2 cups of water. Bring the mixture to a simmer and cook it, covered, for one hour and 15 minutes. Remove the cover and continue simmering the chili until the beans are tender — approximately 15 minutes more.

Ladle the chili into six individual bowls and top it with the remaining ½ cup of tomatoes or tomatillos and the grated cheese.

SUGGESTED ACCOMPANIMENT: *corn salad.*

card the water. Place the squash upside down on a towel to drain. When they cool enough to handle, scoop out the flesh with a spoon, forming shells with walls approximately ¼ inch thick. Add the squash flesh to the stuffing and stir to mix it in thoroughly.

Divide the stuffing among the four squash shells. Sprinkle a little of the remaining Parmesan cheese on top of each squash. Return the squash to the baking dish, and bake them until they are hot — about 30 minutes. Serve the stuffed squash immediately.

SUGGESTED ACCOMPANIMENTS: *green salad; sourdough rolls.*

Lamb-and-Vegetable-Stuffed Acorn Squash

Serves 4
Working time: about 1 hour
Total time: about 2 hours and 30 minutes

Calories **325**
Protein **26g.**
Cholesterol **71mg.**
Total fat **11g.**
Saturated fat **4g.**
Sodium **315mg.**

1 lb. lean lamb (from the leg or loin), trimmed of fat and ground (box, page 8)
4 acorn squash (about 1 lb. each)
1 tsp. safflower oil
½ cup green beans, trimmed and cut into ¼-inch pieces
½ cup fresh corn kernels (cut from one small ear) or frozen corn kernels, thawed
1 onion, chopped
⅓ cup freshly grated Parmesan cheese (about 1 oz.)
¼ tsp. salt
freshly ground black pepper

Preheat the oven to 400° F.

Cut a ½-inch-thick slice from the bottom of each squash so that it will stand upright. Cut a 1-inch-thick slice from the stem end of each squash and scoop out the seeds with a spoon. Set the squash, stem sides down, in a baking dish. Pour 1 cup of water into the dish, then cover it tightly with aluminum foil. Bake the squash until they are tender when pierced with the tip of a sharp knife — about one hour.

While the squash are baking, make the lamb-and-vegetable stuffing. Heat the oil in a large, nonstick skillet over medium-high heat. Add the beans, corn and onion, and sauté them until the onion is soft and lightly browned — about five minutes. Transfer the vegetables to a large bowl. Increase the heat under the skillet to high; add the lamb, and cook it, stirring and breaking it up with a wooden spoon, until it is evenly browned — about five minutes. Pour off any fat. Add the meat to the vegetables and stir in half of the Parmesan cheese, the salt and a generous grinding of pepper. Set the stuffing aside.

Remove the squash from the baking dish and dis-

Polenta Lasagne with Ground Lamb

Serves 8
Working time: about 1 hour and 45 minutes
Total time: about 2 hours and 30 minutes

Calories **345**
Protein **25g.**
Cholesterol **46mg.**
Total fat **9g.**
Saturated fat **4g.**
Sodium **385mg.**

1 lb. lean lamb (from the leg or loin), trimmed of fat and ground (box, page 8)
¼ tsp. salt
2 cups cornmeal
1 tsp. safflower oil
2 onions, finely chopped
6 garlic cloves, finely chopped
56 oz. canned unsalted whole tomatoes, crushed with their juice
2 tbsp. chopped fresh sage, or 2 tsp. dried sage, crumbled
2 tbsp. chopped fresh parsley
2 lb. fresh spinach, stemmed and washed, or 20 oz. frozen spinach, thawed
⅔ cup freshly grated Parmesan cheese
½ cup part-skim grated mozzarella

Bring 8 cups of water to a boil in a large saucepan set over medium-high heat; add the salt. Stirring the water constantly with a wooden spoon, pour in the cornmeal in a slow, steady stream. Reduce the heat to low and simmer the polenta, stirring frequently, until it is thick — about 15 minutes. Spread the polenta on two lightly oiled baking sheets, each 12 by 18 inches. Set the polenta aside to cool while you prepare the lasagne filling.

Heat the oil in a large, nonstick skillet over medium-high heat. Add the onions and garlic and immediately cover the skillet. Reduce the heat to low, and cook the onions and garlic until the onions are translucent — five to eight minutes.

Uncover the skillet and increase the heat to high. Add the ground lamb and sauté it until it has browned, stirring constantly to break the lamb into small pieces. Add the tomatoes and sage, then reduce the heat, and simmer the sauce until it is thick — about one hour. Stir the parsley into the sauce and set it aside.

While the sauce is simmering, prepare the spinach. If you are using fresh spinach, place it, with just the water that clings to its leaves, in a large pot. Cover the pot and steam the spinach over medium heat until it is wilted — two to three minutes. Drain the spinach; when it is cool enough to handle, squeeze the excess liquid from it with your hands. Coarsely chop the spinach and set it aside. If you are using frozen spinach, squeeze the liquid from it, chop it, and set it aside.

Preheat the oven to 400° F. Spread a little of the sauce in the bottom of an 8-by-11-inch baking dish. Trim the sheets of polenta into two 8-by-10-inch rectangles. Set the trimmings in the baking dish. Cover the polenta trimmings with about one third of the remaining sauce. Scatter half of the spinach and half of the Parmesan cheese over the sauce, then finish this layer by spreading about one third of the mozzarella over the top.

Set one of the trimmed polenta sheets atop the mozzarella. Cover the polenta sheet with about half of the remaining sauce, then the remaining spinach, and finally about half of the remaining mozzarella, as in the photograph. Place the other sheet of polenta on top, and spread the remaining sauce and cheeses over it.

Bake the lasagne until the cheese is melted and the lasagne is hot throughout — about 40 minutes. Let the lasagne stand for 10 minutes before serving.

SUGGESTED ACCOMPANIMENT: *a salad of sliced cucumber and red pepper.*

3 *Green peppercorns, garlic and parsley enliven a beef roast that was braised on a bed of mushrooms and onions in the microwave oven (recipe, page 121).*

Microwaving Beef and Lamb

A microwave oven encourages invention — and never more so, perhaps, than in the case of beef and lamb, for the meat may be prepared successfully in any number of ways. Sealed in an oven-cooking bag and microwaved on medium power, for example, a roast braises in its own juices. It might also be sliced into strips for a dish that looks and tastes like a stir fry with very little oil, or cut into cubes and threaded onto wooden skewers for presentation as kebabs.

Particular success attends recipes based on ground meat. The moussaka on page 134 features ground lamb, while a Latin American *picadillo (recipe, page 122)* highlights ground beef combined with raisins and olives. There is even a wholesome, homemade version of the meatball sub *(page 129)*.

A few simple techniques ensure success. Cutting beef or lamb into smaller pieces helps it cook more evenly in the microwave oven, but roasts can also be cooked whole. To keep the meat from drying out, cover the roast during cooking. Avoid salting the roast beforehand — this tends to toughen the meat and leach natural salts and moisture. Chops, too, lend themselves to the microwave process; for best results, lamb chops should be cooked uncovered and turned halfway through the cooking time.

For the sake of succulence, tender cuts of beef and lamb — including patties and meatballs — should be microwaved on high (100 percent power). Less tender cuts, such as those from beef round, should be tightly covered and then simmered in liquid on medium (50 percent power).

Because food continues to cook after it emerges from the microwave oven, achieving the desired degree of doneness involves "standing time." Remove a roast from the oven slightly before the meat looks cooked, then insert an instant-reading thermometer in the center and let the meat stand until it reaches the proper internal temperature. In general, the standing time equals one third to one half the cooking time; wherever such a step is required, the recipe instructions specify how long.

Anticipating that the resourceful cook will wish to compensate for the microwave's inability to brown meat, the following recipes offer a variety of colorful garnishes, from the simplicity of sprinkled paprika to the elegance of a green-peppercorn *persillade*.

Beef Braised on Mushrooms with Green-Peppercorn Persillade

Serves 6
Working time: about 30 minutes
Total time: about 1 hour

Calories **200**
Protein **25g.**
Cholesterol **62mg.**
Total fat **7g.**
Saturated fat **2g.**
Sodium **140mg.**

one 1¾-lb. rump roast, trimmed of fat
1 lb. fresh mushrooms, wiped clean and thinly sliced
1 onion, finely chopped
1 tsp. safflower oil
2 tsp. green peppercorns, rinsed
½ cup parsley leaves
3 garlic cloves
¼ tsp. salt
2 tbsp. flour

Combine the mushrooms, onion and oil in an 8-inch-square baking dish. Cover the dish with heavy-duty plastic wrap and microwave the vegetables on high for five minutes.

While the mushrooms are cooking, prepare the green-peppercorn persillade. Place the green peppercorns, parsley and garlic on a cutting board and sprinkle them with the salt; finely chop the mixture.

Pierce the roast in about 15 places with the tip of a small knife. Press some of the persillade into each of the incisions. Rub any remaining persillade on the outside of the roast.

When the mushrooms have finished cooking, stir the flour into them. Set the roast on top of the mushrooms and cover the dish once again. Cook the meat on medium (50 percent power) for 14 to 16 minutes for medium-rare meat. Let the roast stand, still covered, an additional 10 minutes before carving. (At this point, the internal temperature of the meat should have risen to 145° F.; if it has not, microwave the roast on high for two to three minutes more.)

Cut the roast into very thin slices; divide the meat and mushrooms among six warmed dinner plates. Serve immediately.

SUGGESTED ACCOMPANIMENT: *steamed potatoes and carrots.*

Picadillo

THIS ADAPTATION OF A LATIN AMERICAN FAVORITE
FEATURES RAISINS, OLIVES AND CHICK-PEAS IN ADDITION
TO THE CHOPPED MEAT.

Serves 6
Working time: about 45 minutes
Total time: about 3 hours (includes soaking)

Calories **225**
Protein **18g.**
Cholesterol **35mg.**
Total fat **6g.**
Saturated fat **1g.**
Sodium **235mg.**

1 lb. beef round, trimmed of fat and ground (box, page 8)
1 cup dried chick-peas, picked over
1 onion, chopped
4 garlic cloves, finely chopped
1 tsp. safflower oil
28 oz. canned unsalted whole tomatoes, drained and crushed
½ cup golden raisins
12 pitted green olives, rinsed
½ tsp. cinnamon
½ tsp. allspice
¼ tsp. cayenne pepper
2 bay leaves

Rinse the chick-peas under cold running water, then put them into a large, heavy-bottomed pot with enough water to cover them by about 3 inches. Cover the pot, leaving the lid ajar, and slowly bring the liquid to a boil over medium-low heat on the stove top. Boil the chick-peas for two minutes, then turn off the heat, and soak the chick-peas, covered, for at least one hour. Return the chick-peas to a boil, reduce the heat, and simmer them until they are tender — about one hour.

Combine the onion, garlic and safflower oil in a large bowl. Cover the bowl with plastic wrap and microwave the vegetables on high for four minutes. Add the beef and cook the mixture, uncovered, on medium (50 percent power) for five minutes. Stir the beef, breaking it into small pieces, and cook it on medium for three minutes more.

Drain the chick-peas and add them to the beef mixture. Stir in the tomatoes, raisins, olives, cinnamon, allspice, cayenne pepper and bay leaves. Cook the picadillo, uncovered, on high for 15 minutes, stirring it every five minutes. Remove the bay leaves and let the picadillo stand for five minutes before serving.

SUGGESTED ACCOMPANIMENT: *rice with sweet red pepper.*
EDITOR'S NOTE: *Canned chick-peas can be used in this recipe, thus greatly reducing the cooking time, but the sodium content of the dish will be increased.*

Meatballs in Caper Sauce

Serves 4 as an appetizer
Working time: about 20 minutes
Total time: about 30 minutes

Calories **120**
Protein **14g.**
Cholesterol **34mg.**
Total fat **4g.**
Saturated fat **1g.**
Sodium **190mg.**

10 oz. beef round, trimmed of fat and ground (box, page 8)
1 small onion, chopped
1 cup unsalted brown stock or unsalted chicken stock (recipes, page 137)
¼ cup rolled oats
1 tbsp. chopped fresh parsley
¼ tsp. grated nutmeg
grated zest of 1 lemon
freshly ground black pepper
1 tsp. cornstarch, mixed with 1 tbsp. water
1 tbsp. plain low-fat yogurt
1 tsp. sour cream
1 tsp. capers, rinsed and chopped

Put the onion in a 1-quart baking dish. Cover the dish and microwave the onion on high for three minutes. Transfer the onion to a bowl. Pour the stock into the baking dish and cook it on high until it comes to a simmer — about four minutes.

While the stock is heating, add the beef, rolled oats, ½ tablespoon of the parsley, the nutmeg, the lemon zest and a liberal grinding of pepper to the onion. Knead the mixture to mix it well, then form it into 16 meatballs. Drop the meatballs into the heated stock and cook them covered on high for four minutes.

Using a slotted spoon, transfer the meatballs to a serving dish. Discard all but ½ cup of the cooking liquid in the baking dish; stir the cornstarch mixture into the remaining liquid. Cook the mixture on high until it thickens — about 30 seconds. Let the thickened stock cool for one minute, then stir in the yogurt, sour cream, capers and the remaining ½ tablespoon of parsley. Pour the sauce over the meatballs and serve them while they are still hot.

Beef with Lentils and Sweet Potatoes

Serves 8
Working time: about 20 minutes
Total time: about 1 hour

Calories **365**
Protein **28g.**
Cholesterol **48mg.**
Total fat **6g.**
Saturated fat **2g.**
Sodium **205mg.**

1½ lb. top round steak, trimmed of fat and cut into ¾-inch cubes
1½ cups lentils, picked over and rinsed
2 cups chopped onion
2 garlic cloves, finely chopped
1 tbsp. fresh thyme, or ¾ tsp. dried thyme leaves
½ tsp. anise seeds
¼ tsp. ground cloves
½ tsp. salt
freshly ground black pepper
2 cups unsalted brown stock or unsalted chicken stock (recipes, page 137)
2 lb. sweet potatoes, peeled and cut into ¾ inch cubes
½ cup fresh orange juice
1 tbsp. fresh lemon juice
thyme sprigs for garnish (optional)

In a 3-quart baking dish with a lid, combine the lentils with 1 cup of the chopped onion, the garlic, thyme, anise seeds, cloves, salt and some pepper. Stir in 1½ cups of the stock and 1¼ cups of water. Cover the dish and microwave the mixture on high for 15 minutes, stirring once halfway through the cooking time. Remove the dish from the oven and let the lentil mixture stand while you prepare the sweet potatoes.

Pour the remaining ½ cup of stock into a 2-quart glass bowl; add the remaining cup of onions and the sweet potatoes. Stir the mixture well and then cover the bowl with plastic wrap. Cook the sweet potato mixture on high for 12 minutes, stirring once midway through the cooking time. Remove the bowl from the oven and set it aside.

Stir the beef cubes into the lentil mixture. Cover the dish and cook it on medium high (70 percent power) for eight minutes, stirring once halfway through the cooking time. Remove the dish from the oven and let it stand while you make the sweet potato purée.

Put the sweet potato mixture into a food processor or a blender. Add the orange juice, lemon juice and some pepper; purée the mixture. Transfer the sweet potato purée to a large, deep serving dish and make a well in the center of the purée. Spoon the beef-lentil mixture into the well and, if you like, garnish the dish with a sprig or two of thyme. Serve at once.

SUGGESTED ACCOMPANIMENT: *a salad of cabbage, carrots and raisins.*

Spaghetti Squash with Sherry-Beef Sauce

Serves 4
Working time: about 25 minutes
Total time: about 45 minutes

Calories **250**
Protein **24g.**
Cholesterol **55mg.**
Total fat **6g.**
Saturated fat **2g.**
Sodium **235mg.**

1 lb. beef round, trimmed of fat and ground (box, page 8)
1 spaghetti squash (about 2¾ lb.)
1 small onion, finely chopped
2 garlic cloves, finely chopped
14 oz. canned unsalted whole tomatoes and their juice, puréed in a food processor or a blender
2 oz. fresh mushrooms, wiped clean, trimmed and sliced (about ¾ cup)
½ cup dry sherry
1 tbsp. brown sugar
1½ tsp. chopped fresh oregano, or ½ tsp. dried oregano
¼ tsp. salt
freshly ground black pepper
2 tbsp. freshly grated Parmesan cheese
several parsley sprigs (optional)

Pierce the squash in several places with a fork to allow steam to escape during cooking. Place the squash in a baking dish and microwave it on high for 10 minutes. Turn the squash over and cook it on high for six minutes more. Remove the squash from the oven and let it stand while you prepare the sauce.

Crumble the ground beef into a hard plastic colander set in a 2-quart bowl. Sprinkle the onion and garlic over the beef. Cook the beef, onion and garlic on high for six minutes, stirring them midway through the cooking time. Discard the liquid that collected in the bowl; transfer the beef mixture to the bowl.

Stir the tomatoes, mushrooms, sherry, brown sugar, oregano, salt and some pepper into the beef mixture. Cook the sauce uncovered on high for 10 minutes.

About five minutes before the sauce finishes cooking, slice the squash crosswise into rounds about 3 inches thick. Scoop out and discard the seeds and loose fibers. Using a fork, scrape out the spaghetti-like strands of flesh and mound them on a serving platter. Top the squash with some of the sauce, the Parmesan cheese and, if desired, the parsley sprigs. Pour the remaining sauce into a sauceboat and pass it separately.

SUGGESTED ACCOMPANIMENT: *red-leaf lettuce salad.*

Lime-Ginger Beef

Serves 4
Working time: about 25 minutes
Total time: about 45 minutes

Calories **240**
Protein **25g.**
Cholesterol **65mg.**
Total fat **10g.**
Saturated fat **3g.**
Sodium **180mg.**

2 top loin steaks (about 10 oz. each), trimmed of fat and cut into thin strips
freshly ground black pepper
1 tbsp. safflower oil
2 scallions, trimmed and sliced into thin strips
1 large carrot, julienned
1 sweet red pepper, seeded, deribbed and julienned
Lime-ginger sauce
grated zest and juice of 1 lime
1 tsp. grated fresh ginger
2 tbsp. dry sherry
2 tsp. low-sodium soy sauce
½ tsp. finely chopped garlic
1 tbsp. sugar
1 tbsp. cornstarch, mixed with ¼ cup water

Preheat a microwave browning dish on high for the maximum time allowed in the dish's instruction manual. While the dish is heating, combine all the ingredients for the lime-ginger sauce in a small bowl. Set the bowl aside. Season the beef strips with a generous grinding of black pepper.

When the browning dish is heated, brush ½ tablespoon of the oil evenly over the dish to coat it. Sear half of the beef strips on the dish, stirring and turning the meat with a wooden spoon. Once the beef has been seared — after one or two minutes — transfer it to a baking dish. Wipe off the browning dish with a paper towel and reheat it for three minutes. Brush the remaining ½ tablespoon of oil onto the dish and sear the remaining beef the same way. Add the beef to the baking dish.

Add the scallions, carrot and red pepper to the beef. Pour the sauce over all and microwave the mixture on high for three minutes. Serve the beef and vegetables from the baking dish or transfer them to a platter; serve at once.

SUGGESTED ACCOMPANIMENT: *steamed rice.*

Layered Beef and Potato Cake

Serves 8
Working time: about 45 minutes
Total time: about 1 hour and 15 minutes

Calories **260**
Protein **27g.**
Cholesterol **67mg.**
Total fat **6g.**
Saturated fat **2g.**
Sodium **260mg.**

2¼ lb. beef round, trimmed of fat and ground (box, page 8)
6 garlic cloves, finely chopped
½ cup chopped fresh mint, or ¼ cup dried mint
¼ cup chopped fresh parsley
¾ tsp. salt
freshly ground black pepper
2 lb. baking potatoes, peeled and thinly sliced
½ cup unsalted brown stock or unsalted chicken stock (recipes, page 137)

Combine the beef, garlic, mint, parsley, salt and some pepper in a bowl and set the bowl aside.

Cover the bottom of a 2-quart round casserole with a layer of overlapping potato slices. Scatter about ¼ of the beef mixture over the potatoes and then gently press the meat onto the potatoes to make a somewhat even layer. Continue the layering process until the beef mixture and the potato slices are used up; there will be about 8 layers. Drizzle the stock over the layered potato-meat cake. Microwave the cake on high for 25 minutes, turning the dish a quarter turn every eight minutes. Let the dish stand for 10 minutes before unmolding the cake onto a serving platter. To serve, cut the cake into eight wedges.

SUGGESTED ACCOMPANIMENT: *a salad of green beans and sweet red peppers.*

Meatball Subs

Serves 6
Working time: about 45 minutes
Total time: about 1 hour and 15 minutes

Calories **290**
Protein **24g.**
Cholesterol **50mg.**
Total fat **8g.**
Saturated fat **2g.**
Sodium **415mg.**

1¼ lb. beef round, trimmed of fat and ground (box, page 8)
2 sweet red peppers, seeded, deribbed and finely chopped
1 green pepper, seeded, deribbed and finely chopped
2 onions, finely chopped
4 garlic cloves, finely chopped
1 tsp. safflower oil
28 oz. canned unsalted whole tomatoes, drained and puréed
2 tbsp. chopped fresh oregano, or 2 tsp. dried oregano
1 tbsp. chopped fresh parsley
2 tsp. fennel seeds
freshly ground black pepper
½ cup dry bread crumbs
¼ tsp. salt
3 submarine rolls, halved and split lengthwise, leaving the halves hinged on one side
¼ cup freshly grated Parmesan cheese

Combine the peppers, onions, garlic and oil in a large bowl. Cover the bowl and microwave it on high for eight minutes. Let the bowl stand for two minutes before uncovering it. Add the tomatoes to the bowl. Cook the sauce, uncovered, on high for 25 minutes.

While the sauce is cooking, make the meatballs. In a bowl, knead together the beef, oregano, parsley, fennel seeds, some black pepper, the bread crumbs and the salt. Form the mixture into 12 meatballs.

Immerse the meatballs in the tomato sauce and cook them, covered, on medium high (70 percent power) for eight minutes, stirring halfway through the cooking time. Let the meatballs and sauce stand for five minutes.

Place two meatballs in each of the submarine roll halves. Spoon some sauce on top of the meatballs and sprinkle them with the Parmesan cheese. Serve the extra sauce alongside.

Beef Tenderloin Kebabs with Tomato Sauce

Serves 4
Working time: about 25 minutes
Total time: about 40 minutes

Calories **210**
Protein **20g.**
Cholesterol **54mg.**
Total fat **8g.**
Saturated fat **2g.**
Sodium **190mg.**

1 lb. beef tenderloin, trimmed of fat and cut into 1-inch cubes	
1 yellow squash, cut into 1-inch cubes	
12 pearl onions, blanched in boiling water for 2 minutes and peeled	
1 tsp. safflower oil	

Tomato sauce

¼ cup finely chopped onion	
1 garlic clove, finely chopped	
1 tsp. safflower oil	
¼ tsp. dry mustard	
1 tsp. cider vinegar	
14 oz. canned unsalted whole tomatoes, drained and chopped	
1 tbsp. honey	
¼ tsp. salt	
freshly ground black pepper	

To prepare the sauce, combine the onion, garlic and oil in a 1-quart bowl. Cover the bowl with plastic wrap and microwave the mixture on high for one minute. Dissolve the dry mustard in the vinegar and add it, along with the tomatoes, honey, salt and some pepper, to the onion mixture. Cover the bowl and cook the sauce on high for two minutes; let the sauce stand covered while you prepare the kebabs.

Preheat the microwave browning grill for the maximum time allowed in the grill's instruction manual. Meanwhile, assemble the kebabs by alternating the beef, squash and onions on wooden skewers. Brush the grill with the oil. Set the kebabs on the grill, leaving a 1-inch space between them. Cook the kebabs on high for two minutes; turn them over and cook them for two minutes more.

Transfer the kebabs to a microwave-safe serving platter. Spoon the sauce over the kebabs and cook them on medium high (70 percent power) to heat the sauce — about two minutes before serving the kebabs.

SUGGESTED ACCOMPANIMENT: *spinach fettuccine.*

Onions Stuffed with Ground Beef and Swiss Chard

Serves 6 as a luncheon entrée
Working time: about 45 minutes
Total time: about 1 hour and 15 minutes

Calories **170**
Protein **17g.**
Cholesterol **28mg.**
Total fat **3g.**
Saturated fat **1g.**
Sodium **350mg.**

¾ lb. beef round, trimmed of fat and ground (box, page 8)
6 onions (about 2½ lb.), unpeeled
¼ lb. fresh mushrooms, wiped clean and finely chopped
1 lb. Swiss chard or fresh spinach, stemmed and washed
½ cup low-fat cottage cheese, sieved
¼ cup dry bread crumbs
¼ tsp. salt
freshly ground black pepper
grated zest of 2 lemons
2 garlic cloves, finely chopped
1 tbsp. chopped fresh parsley

Cut off and discard ½ inch from the top of each onion. Place the onions in a baking dish, cover the dish with heavy-duty plastic wrap, and microwave the onions on high until they are very tender — about 10 minutes. Set them aside to cool.

Place the mushrooms in a 2-quart bowl, cover it with plastic wrap, and cook the mushrooms on high for six minutes. Transfer the mushrooms to another bowl.

Add the Swiss chard or spinach to the 2-quart bowl and cook the greens on high until they wilt — two to three minutes. Drain the greens, squeeze as much liquid from them as possible with your hands, and chop them fine. Add the greens to the mushrooms.

Peel the cooked onions and, using a small spoon or your fingers, remove the centers of the onions. Chop enough of the centers to produce ½ cup and add this to the mushrooms and greens. Stir in the beef, cottage cheese, bread crumbs, salt and some pepper.

Fill the onion shells with the meat mixture and stand them upright in the baking dish; cover the onions loosely with wax paper. Cook the stuffed onions on medium high (70 percent power) for six minutes, rotating the dish a half turn midway through the cooking time. Remove the onions from the oven and let them stand for three minutes.

Mix the zest, garlic and parsley in a small bowl, sprinkle the mixture over the onions, and serve them hot.

SUGGESTED ACCOMPANIMENT: *tomato salad.*

Lamb Roast with Winter Vegetables

Serves 8
Working time: about 30 minutes
Total time: about 1 hour

Calories **220**
Protein **26g.**
Cholesterol **75mg.**
Total fat **8g.**
Saturated fat **3g.**
Sodium **175mg.**

one 4-lb. leg of lamb, sirloin half, trimmed of fat, boned and tied (technique, page 105)
2 tsp. chili powder
1 tbsp. chopped fresh rosemary, or 2 tsp. dried rosemary, crumbled
freshly ground black pepper
1 small cauliflower (about 1¼ lb.), trimmed and divided into florets
3 carrots, sliced on the diagonal into 1-inch pieces
1 lb. Brussels sprouts, trimmed
⅔ cup unsalted brown stock or unsalted chicken stock (recipes, page 137)
¼ tsp. salt
1 tbsp. cornstarch, mixed with 2 tbsp. water

With your fingers, rub the chili powder over the outside of the roast, then sprinkle it with the rosemary and a generous grinding of pepper. Place the lamb in an oven cooking bag and loosely tie the bag with string or a strip of plastic wrap, leaving an opening for steam to escape. Make sure that the opening faces upward so that the cooking juices do not run out. Place the roast in a shallow dish.

Microwave the roast on medium (50 percent power) for 16 minutes. Rotate the dish 180 degrees, then turn the lamb over, taking care to keep the juices in the bag; cook the lamb for 16 minutes more.

While the lamb is roasting, pour enough water into a large pot to fill it about 1 inch deep. Set a vegetable steamer in the pot; put the cauliflower, carrots and Brussels sprouts into the steamer and cover the pot. Set the pot aside.

Remove the lamb from the oven and take it out of the roasting bag. Let the roast stand for 10 minutes. Pour the juices that have collected in the bag into a 1-quart bowl. Set the bowl aside. (At this point an instant-reading meat thermometer inserted into the center of the roast should register 145° F.; if it does not, microwave the lamb for another five minutes at medium power.)

While the roast is resting, bring the water in the pot to a boil on the stove top and steam the vegetables until they are tender — seven to 10 minutes.

To make the sauce, skim the fat off the top of the liquid in the bowl. Stir the stock, the salt and the cornstarch mixture into the juices. Microwave the sauce on high until it has thickened — about two minutes. Stir it once again.

Slice the meat, arrange it on a platter surrounded by the vegetables, and pour the sauce over all.

SUGGESTED ACCOMPANIMENT: *whole-wheat dinner rolls.*

Lamb Baked in Saffron Yogurt

Serves 4
Working time: about 30 minutes
Total time: about 4 hours and 45 minutes
(includes marinating)

Calories **195**
Protein **25g.**
Cholesterol **78mg.**
Total fat **8g.**
Saturated fat **3g.**
Sodium **90mg.**

1¼ lb. lean lamb (from the leg or loin), trimmed of fat and cut into 1-inch cubes
3 garlic cloves, finely chopped
2 tbsp. finely chopped fresh ginger
¼ tsp. saffron threads or turmeric
1 tbsp. cornstarch
1 jalapeño pepper, seeded, deribbed and finely chopped (caution, page 23)
¾ cup plain low-fat yogurt
4 radishes, thinly sliced, for garnish
2 scallions, trimmed and thinly sliced, for garnish

Mix the lamb cubes, garlic, ginger, saffron or turmeric, cornstarch, jalapeño pepper and yogurt in a baking dish. Cover the dish and refrigerate it for four hours.

Microwave the lamb and its marinade, covered with wax paper, on medium (50 percent power) for 15 minutes, stirring the mixture every five minutes. Let the dish stand for five minutes; stir it once again before serving. Garnish the lamb with the radishes and scallions before serving.

SUGGESTED ACCOMPANIMENTS: *yellow rice; green beans.*
EDITOR'S NOTE: *Do not marinate the lamb cubes for more than six hours; they will become too soft.*

Moussaka

THIS IS A LIGHTER VERSION OF THE TRADITIONAL
GREEK LAMB AND EGGPLANT DISH.

Serves 6
Working time: about 30 minutes
Total time: about 1 hour

Calories **260**
Protein **22g.**
Cholesterol **57mg.**
Total fat **10g.**
Saturated fat **4g.**
Sodium **295mg.**

1¼ lb. lean lamb (from the leg or loin), trimmed of fat and ground (box, page 8)	
1 large eggplant (about 1½ lb.)	
3 tbsp. chopped fresh basil, or 1 tbsp. dried basil	
¼ cup unsalted brown stock or unsalted chicken stock (recipes, page 137)	
1 onion, thinly sliced	
2 garlic cloves, finely chopped	
¼ tsp. salt	
freshly ground black pepper	
1 zucchini, ends trimmed, grated	

14 oz. canned unsalted whole tomatoes, seeded and coarsely chopped	
1 tbsp. safflower oil	
¼ cup flour	
1 cup low-fat milk	
⅓ cup freshly grated Parmesan cheese (about 1 oz.)	
½ cup fresh bread crumbs	

Slice the eggplant into ¼-inch-thick slices. Arrange some of the eggplant slices in a single layer on a large plate. Sprinkle some of the basil over the eggplant and continue the layering process until all of the eggplant and basil are used up. Drizzle the stock over the layered eggplant. Cover the plate with heavy-duty plastic wrap and microwave the eggplant on high for four minutes. Let the eggplant stand for five minutes; pour the juice that accumulates on the plate into a small bowl and set it aside.

While the eggplant is resting, crumble the lamb into

a 2-quart bowl. Add the onion, garlic, salt and some pepper to the lamb and toss the mixture well. Microwave the lamb mixture on high for two minutes. Stir in all but 1 tablespoon of the zucchini and all but 2 tablespoons of the tomatoes and then cook the mixture on high for three minutes more. Set the bowl aside.

Mix the oil and flour in a small bowl. Microwave the mixture on high for 45 seconds. Stir ¼ cup of the milk into the flour mixture, then pour in the remaining milk in a steady stream, stirring constantly until the mixture is smooth. Stir in the Parmesan cheese and microwave the sauce on high until it thickens — about two minutes. Whisk in ¼ cup of the reserved juice from the cooked eggplant and set the sauce aside.

To assemble the moussaka, line the bottom of an 8-inch-square baking dish with one fourth of the eggplant slices. Drain the meat-zucchini mixture, discarding the juices, then stir in the breadcrumbs. Spoon ⅓ of this mixture over the eggplant. Dab a few tablespoons of the sauce onto the meat mixture. Make two more layers of eggplant, meat and sauce. Arrange the remaining eggplant slices on top, then cover the eggplant with the rest of the sauce. Sprinkle the reserved zucchini and tomato over the moussaka. Microwave the dish uncovered on high for 15 minutes. Let the moussaka stand for 10 minutes and then drain any liquid that has accumulated in the dish. Cut the moussaka into six portions and serve.

SUGGESTED ACCOMPANIMENT: *orzo with mushrooms.*

Sage-Marinated Lamb Chops

Serves 4
Working time: about 25 minutes
Total time: about 1 hour and 20 minutes
(includes marinating)

Calories **154**
Protein **18g.**
Cholesterol **55mg.**
Total fat **5g.**
Saturated fat **2g.**
Sodium **185mg.**

8 lamb loin chops (about 2 lb.), trimmed of fat
2 tsp. chopped fresh sage, or ¾ tsp. crumbled dried sage
3 garlic cloves, finely chopped
grated zest of 1 lemon
2 tbsp. balsamic vinegar, or 1½ tbsp. red wine vinegar mixed with ½ tsp. honey
1 tbsp. dark brown sugar
1 tbsp. brandy
¼ tsp. salt
freshly ground black pepper

Mix the sage, garlic, lemon zest, vinegar, brown sugar, brandy, salt and some pepper in an 8-inch-square glass dish. Add the lamb chops to the dish and turn them to coat them with the marinade. Let the lamb chops stand for 1 hour at room temperature; turn the chops every 15 minutes while they marinate.

Microwave the chops, uncovered, on high for two minutes. Rotate the dish 180 degrees. Turn the chops over, rearranging them so that the chops that were at the outside are now at the center. Cook the chops on high for three minutes more. Remove the dish from the oven and loosely cover it with aluminum foil. Let the lamb chops stand for five minutes before serving them.

SUGGESTED ACCOMPANIMENTS: *stewed tomatoes; steamed new potatoes.*

Lamb Meat Loaf with Olives

Serves 6
Working time: about 15 minutes
Total time: about 30 minutes

Calories **225**
Protein **28g.**
Cholesterol **86mg.**
Total fat **9g.**
Saturated fat **3g.**
Sodium **225mg.**

1¾ lb. lean lamb (from the leg or loin), trimmed of fat and ground (box, page 8)
1 egg white, lightly beaten
1 tbsp. chopped fresh oregano, or 1 tsp. dried oregano
¼ tsp. cayenne pepper
2 garlic cloves, finely chopped
¼ cup finely chopped onion
3 cups fresh parsley, chopped
6 oil-cured black olives, pitted and finely chopped
⅓ cup dry bread crumbs
¼ cup freshly grated Romano or Parmesan cheese (about ½ oz.)
1 tbsp. red wine vinegar
1½ tbsp. tomato paste

In a large bowl, combine the egg white, oregano, cayenne pepper, garlic and onion. Add the lamb, parsley, olives, bread crumbs, cheese, vinegar and 1 tablespoon of the tomato paste; mix all of the ingredients with a wooden spoon until they are well combined.

Shape the meat mixture into a log about 3 inches in diameter. Place the log in a shallow baking dish and spread the remaining ½ tablespoon of tomato paste over the meat's surface. Cook the loaf, uncovered, on high for 10 to 12 minutes, rotating the dish a half turn midway through the cooking time. Let the meat loaf stand for 10 minutes before slicing it into 12 pieces.

SUGGESTED ACCOMPANIMENTS: *butternut squash; green peas.*

Making your own stock is easy enough, and the recipes that follow tell you how. Canned chicken stock may be substituted, but look for the low-sodium kind; if you cannot get it, eliminate the salt from the recipe you are preparing. Canned beef stock is very salty and does not have the quality of brown stock; again, if you must use it, be sure to leave out the salt in the recipe.

Chicken Stock

Makes about 2 quarts
Working time: about 20 minutes
Total time: about 3 hours

5 lb. uncooked chicken trimmings and bones, the bones cracked with a heavy knife
2 carrots, cut into ½-inch-thick rounds
2 celery stalks, cut into 1-inch pieces
2 large onions (about 1 lb.), cut in half, one half stuck with 2 cloves
2 fresh thyme sprigs, or ½ tsp. dried thyme leaves
1 or 2 bay leaves
10 to 15 parsley stems
5 black peppercorns

Put the chicken trimmings and bones into a heavy stockpot; pour in enough water to cover them by about 2 inches. Bring the liquid to a boil over medium heat, skimming off the scum that rises to the surface. Reduce the heat and simmer the liquid for 10 minutes, skimming and adding a little cold water to help precipitate the scum.

Add the vegetables, herbs and peppercorns, and submerge them in the liquid. If necessary, pour in enough additional water to cover the contents of the pot. Simmer the stock for two to three hours, skimming as necessary to remove the scum.

Strain the stock and discard the solids. Allow the stock to stand until it is tepid, then refrigerate it overnight to allow the fat to congeal. Spoon off and discard the layer of fat.

Tightly covered and refrigerated, the stock may be safely kept for two or three days. Stored in small, tightly covered freezer containers and frozen, the stock may be kept for as long as six months.

EDITOR'S NOTE: *The chicken gizzard and heart may be added to the stock. Wings and necks — rich in natural gelatin — produce a particularly gelatinous stock, ideal for sauces and jellied dishes. The liver should never be used.*

Brown Stock

Makes about 3 quarts
Working time: about 40 minutes
Total time: about 5½ hours

3 lb. veal breast (or veal-shank or beef-shank meat), cut into 3-inch pieces
3 lb. uncooked veal or beef bones, cracked
2 onions, quartered
2 celery stalks, chopped
2 carrots, sliced
3 unpeeled garlic cloves, crushed
8 black peppercorns
3 cloves
2 tsp. fresh thyme, or ½ tsp. dried thyme leaves
1 bay leaf

Preheat the oven to 425° F. Place the meat, bones, onions, celery and carrots in a large roasting pan and roast them in the oven until they are well browned — about one hour.

Transfer the contents of the roasting pan to a large pot. Pour 2 cups of water into the roasting pan; with a spatula, scrape up the browned bits from the bottom of the pan. Pour the liquid into the pot.

Add the garlic, peppercorns and cloves. Pour in enough water to cover the contents of the pot by about 3 inches. Bring the liquid to a boil, then reduce the heat to maintain a slow simmer, and skim any impurities from the surface. Add the thyme and bay leaf, then simmer the stock very gently for four hours, skimming occasionally during the process.

Strain the stock and discard the solids. Allow the stock to stand until it is tepid, then refrigerate it overnight to allow the fat to congeal. Spoon off and discard the layer of fat.

Tightly covered and refrigerated, the stock may be safely kept for two or three days. Stored in small, tightly covered freezer containers and frozen, the stock may be kept for as long as six months.

EDITOR'S NOTE: *Thoroughly browning the meat, bones and vegetables in the oven should produce a stock with a rich mahogany color. If your stock does not seem dark enough, cook 1 tablespoon of tomato paste in a small pan over medium heat, stirring constantly, until it darkens — about three minutes. Add this to the stock about one hour before the end of the cooking time.*

Any combination of meat and bones may be used to make the stock. Ask your butcher to crack the bones.

Glossary

Arm pot roast: a cut of beef from the lower section of the chuck or shoulder; it is usually braised.

Ancho chili pepper: the ripened and dried form of the poblano chili pepper. Dark reddish brown in color, and mild to slightly hot, the ancho is among the most commonly used chilies in Mexico. See also Chili peppers.

Annatto (also called *achiote*): a natural yellow coloring and flavoring agent ground from the rust-colored seeds of the annatto tree; the seeds are sold whole or ground and can be found in Latin American, Caribbean and East Indian markets.

Balsamic vinegar: an extremely fragrant wine-based vinegar made in Modena, Italy.

Bâtonnet: a vegetable piece that has been cut in the shape of a stick — usually about 1½ inches long and ¼ inch square.

Belgian endive: a small, cigar-shaped vegetable, composed of many tightly wrapped white to pale-yellow leaves, which have a pleasant bitter flavor.

Bottom round: the lean, large muscle found in the outside portion of the beef round. Bottom round is most often cut into roasts and steaks; it can be roasted or braised.

Braise: to cook food with liquid over low heat; it can be done on top of the stove or in the oven. Braising is an excellent cooking method for tenderizing tough cuts of meat.

Bulgur: whole-wheat kernels that have been steamed, dried and cracked.

Butterfly: to split a boneless cut of meat in half horizontally, leaving the halves hinged on one side.

Calorie (or kilocalorie): a unit of heat measurement, used to gauge the amount of energy a food supplies when it is broken down for use in the body.

Capers: the pickled flower buds of the caper plant, a shrub native to the Mediterranean. Capers should be rinsed before use to rid them of excess salt.

Caramelize: to heat sugar, or a naturally sugar-rich food such as onion, until the sugar becomes brown and syrupy.

Cardamom: the bittersweet, aromatic dried seed pods of a plant in the ginger family. Cardamom seeds may be used whole or ground.

Cayenne pepper: a fiery powder ground from the seeds and pods of various red chili peppers.

Chanterelle mushrooms (also called *girolle*): a variety of wild mushroom that is trumpet-shaped and yellow-orange in color. Chanterelles are available fresh or dried; dried chanterelles should be soaked in hot water before use.

Chiffonade: a leafy vegetable sliced into very thin shreds.

Chili paste: a robust, spicy paste made of chili peppers, salt and other ingredients. Numerous kinds are available in Asian markets.

Chili pepper: any of several varieties of red or green pepper with an extremely hot taste. Whether fresh or dried, chili peppers contain volatile oils that can irritate the skin and eyes; they must be handled with the utmost care *(caution, page 23)*.

Chine: the backbone of an animal. Also, to cut through the backbone of a roast that contains part of the chine to make the meat easier to carve after cooking; this is done by the butcher.

Cholesterol: a waxlike substance that is manufactured in the human liver and is also found in foods of animal origin. Although a certain amount of cholesterol is necessary for producing hormones and building cell walls, an excess can accumulate in the arteries, contributing to heart disease. See also Monounsaturated fat; Polyunsaturated fat; Saturated fat.

Cilantro (also called fresh coriander and Chinese parsley): the fresh leaves of the coriander plant; cilantro imparts a lemony, pleasingly pungent flavor to many Latin American, Indian and Asian dishes.

Cornichons: small, French, sour gherkin pickles.

Couscous: a fine-grained semolina pasta, traditionally served as a base for the classic North African stew of the same name.

Crystallized ginger (also called candied ginger): stems of ginger preserved with sugar. Crystallized ginger should not be confused with ginger in syrup.

Daikon radish: a long, white Japanese radish.

Dark sesame oil: a seasoning oil, high in polyunsaturated fats, that is made from toasted sesame seeds. Because dark sesame oil has a relatively low smoking point, it is rarely used for sautéing. Dark sesame oil should not be confused or replaced with lighter sesame cooking oils.

Dijon mustard: a smooth mustard once manufactured only in Dijon, France; it may be flavored with herbs or green peppercorns.

Eye round: a lean oval muscle found within the round of beef; it can be roasted or braised whole, or sliced into thin steaks.

Fat: a basic component of many foods, containing three types of fatty acids — saturated, monounsaturated and polyunsaturated — in varying proportions. See also Monounsaturated fat; Polyunsaturated fat; Saturated fat.

Fennel (also called anise, finochio and Florence fennel): a vegetable with feathery green tops and a thick, white bulbous stalk. It has a milky, licorice flavor and can be eaten raw or cooked.

Fennel seeds: the aromatic dried seeds from herb fennel, a relative of the vegetable fennel; they are used as a licorice-flavored seasoning in many Italian dishes.

Filet mignon: technically, a steak cut from the smaller half of the beef tenderloin.

Ginger: the spicy, buff-colored rhizome, or rootlike stem, of the ginger plant, used as seasoning either in fresh form or dried and powdered. Dried ginger makes a poor substitute for fresh. See also Crystallized ginger.

Grape leaves: the tender, delicately flavored leaves of the grapevine. Grape leaves are used in many Mediterranean cuisines as wrappers for savory fillings. Fresh grape leaves should be cooked for five minutes in boiling water before using them in a recipe; grape leaves packed in brine should be thoroughly rinsed.

Hoisin sauce: a thick, dark reddish brown sauce generally made from soybeans, flour, garlic, sugar and spices.

Instant-reading thermometer: a thermometer that registers the internal temperature of a roast or steak in a matter of seconds.

Jalapeño chili pepper: a squat, green, hot chili pepper, essential to a number of Mexican dishes. See also Chili pepper.

Julienne: to slice food into matchstick-size pieces; also the name for the pieces themselves.

Juniper berries: the dried berries of the juniper tree, used as a key flavoring in gin as well as in meat marinades.

London broil: formerly, this referred only to broiled beef flank steak; today the name applies to a variety of meat cuts, usually boneless, that can be broiled and thinly sliced.

Madeira: a fortified wine from the island of Madeira. It has an underlying burned flavor, which is the result of heating the wine after fermentation.

Marbling: the intramuscular fat that is found within meat. This fat cannot be trimmed away, but much of it can be rendered during cooking.

Marinade: a mixture of aromatic ingredients in which meat is allowed to stand before cooking to enrich its flavor. Some marinades will tenderize meat, but they do not penetrate deeply.

Masa harina: a specially prepared corn flour used chiefly in the making of tortillas.

Monounsaturated fat: one of the three types of fatty acids found in fats. Monounsaturated fats are believed not to raise the level of cholesterol in the blood. Some oils high in monounsaturated fats — olive oil, for example — are thought to lower the blood cholesterol level.

Nappa cabbage (also called Chinese cabbage): an elongated cabbage resembling romaine lettuce, with long, broad ribs and crinkled, light-green to white leaves.

Okra: the green pods of a plant indigenous to Africa, where it is called gumbo. In stews, okra is prized for its thickening properties.

Olive oil: any of various grades of oil extracted from olives. Extra virgin olive oil has a full, fruity flavor and very low acidity. Virgin olive oil is lighter in flavor and slightly higher in acidity. Pure olive oil, a processed blend of olive oils, has the lightest taste and the highest acidity.

Orzo: a rice-shaped dried pasta.

Papaya: a tropical fruit, whose juice contains the enzyme papain; the action of this enzyme breaks down the protein in meat and tenderizes it.

Persillade: a French term for chopped parsley mixed with garlic.

Phyllo (also spelled filo): a Greek pastry dough that is rolled and stretched to tissue-paper thinness. It is usually available frozen.

Pine nuts (also called pignoli): seeds from the cone of the stone pine, a tree native to the Mediterranean. The buttery flavor of pine nuts can be heightened by light toasting.

Polenta: boiled cornmeal, a dish traditionally eaten in Northern Italy.

Polyunsaturated fat: one of the three types of fatty acids found in fat. Polyunsaturated fats exist in abundance in such vegetable oils as safflower, corn or soybean. Polyunsaturated fats lower the level of cholesterol in the blood.

Porcini mushrooms (also called cepes): a variety of fresh or dried wild mushroom with a pungent earthy flavor, often used in Italian cookery. Dried porcini should be soaked in hot water before use.

Port: a sweet fortified wine originally produced in northern Portugal and shipped through the city of Oporto.

Pot roast: a chunky piece of beef cooked by braising.

Primal cut: the divisions of a carcass prepared by wholesalers. The beef primal cuts are the chuck, rib, short loin, sirloin, round, brisket and fore-shank, short plate, and flank. The primal cuts of lamb are the shoulder, rib, loin, sirloin and leg, fore-shank, and breast.

Prosciutto: an air-cured ham that is sliced paper-thin before serving. The best is produced near Parma, Italy.

Recommended Dietary Allowance (RDA): the average required daily amount of an essential nutrient as determined for groups of healthy people of various ages by the National Research Council.

Reduce: to boil down a liquid or sauce in order to concentrate its flavor and thicken its consistency.

Rice vinegar: a mild, fragrant vinegar that is less assertive than cider vinegar or distilled white vinegar. It is available in dark, light, seasoned and sweetened varieties; Japanese rice vinegar generally is milder than the Chinese version.

Round: a wholesale cut of the hindquarter of beef. It contains the top round, bottom round, eye round, tip roast and beef shank.

Rump: the most tender portion of the beef bottom round, close to the sirloin; it is usually roasted.

Safflower oil: the vegetable oil that contains the highest proportion of polyunsaturated fats.

Saffron: the dried, yellowish red stigmas (or threads) of the flower of *Crocus sativus;* saffron yields a pungent flavor and a brilliant yellow color.

Saturated fat: one of the three types of fatty acids present in fats. Found in abundance in animal products and in coconut and palm oils, saturated fats raise the level of blood cholesterol. Because high blood cholesterol levels contribute to heart disease, saturated-fat consumption should be kept to a minimum — preferably less than 10 percent of the calories consumed each day.

Scallopini: cutlets sliced or pounded thin.

Sear: to brown the surface of meat by a short application of intense heat; searing adds flavor and color, but it does not seal in meat juices.

Sesame oil: See Dark sesame oil.

Shallot: a mild variety of onion. If shallots are unavailable, substitute scallions or yellow onions in a recipe.

Shiitake mushrooms: a variety of mushroom, originally cultivated only in Japan, that is sold fresh or dried. The dried form should be soaked and stemmed before use.

Sirloin: in beef, the thick end of the loin, separated from the short loin; it is cut into steaks or roasts, which can be grilled or roasted. In lamb the sirloin is usually left attached to the leg; it is sometimes divided into chops.

Soy sauce: a savory, salty brown liquid made from fermented soybeans. One tablespoon of regular soy sauce contains about 1,030 milligrams of sodium; lower-sodium variations may contain as little as half that amount.

Stir fry: to cook thin pieces of meat or vegetables, or a combination of both, over high heat in a small amount of oil, stirring constantly to ensure even cooking in a short time. The traditional cooking vessel is a Chinese wok; a large, nonstick or heavy-bottomed skillet may also be used.

Stock: a savory broth that is made by simmering aromatic vegetables, herbs, spices, bones and meat trimmings in water. Stock is often used as a flavor-rich liquid for braising meat and making sauces.

Sun-dried tomatoes: tomatoes that have been dried to concentrate their flavor and preserve them; some are then packed in oil. Most sun-dried tomatoes are of Italian origin, but they are now being produced in the United States too.

Sweet chili sauce: any of a group of Asian sauces containing chilies, vinegar, garlic, sugar and salt. Sweet chili sauce may be used as a condiment to accompany meats, poultry or fish, or it may be included as an ingredient in the dish.

Tenderize: to make meat tender by pounding, grinding, or slow cooking in moist heat — or by the use of a substance containing enzymes that break down meat protein.

Tenderloin (also called fillet): the most tender muscle of the carcass, located inside the loin.

Tip: a muscle located in the primal round of beef; it is often sold as sirloin tip roast or as steaks. The tip can be roasted or braised.

Tomatillo: a small, tart, green, tomato-like fruit vegetable that is covered with a loose, papery husk. It is frequently used in Mexican dishes.

Top loin: the larger muscle of the beef short loin; it is sold as steaks or left whole for roasting.

Top round: the inside portion of the beef round; it can be cut into steaks or roasts.

Wheat berries: unpolished, whole wheat kernels with a nutty taste and a chewy texture.

Wild rice: the seeds of a water grass native to the Great Lakes region of North America. Wild rice is appreciated for its robust flavor.

Zest: the flavorful outermost layer of citrus-fruit rind, cut or grated free of the white pith, which lies just beneath it.

Index

Picture Credits

All photographs in this book were taken by staff photographer Renée Comet unless otherwise indicated.

2: top, Scarlet Cheng; center, Carolyn Wall Rothery. 4: lower left, Michael Latil. 5: upper right, Michael Latil. 6: Henry Groskinsky. 9: art by William J. Hennessy, Jr./A & W Graphics, Fairfax, Va. 15: Michael Latil. 16: top, Michael Latil. 17: Lisa Masson. 18: Steven Biver. 19: top, Taran Z; bottom, Michael Latil. 24: Michael Latil. 25: Taran Z. 28: Steven Biver. 29: Lisa Masson. 31: Michael Latil. 35: Steven Biver. 38: Lisa Masson. 42: Michael Latil. 43: Taran Z. 48: top, Michael Latil; bottom, Taran Z. 49: Steven Biver. 55: Steven Biver. 67: top, Michael Latil. 72: top, Michael Latil. 74: Taran Z. 76: Taran Z. 77: Michael Latil. 80: Michael Latil. 89: Taran Z. 92: right, Taran Z. 104: bottom, Taran Z. 105: Taran Z. 111: top, Taran Z. 120: Michael Latil. 124-128: Michael Latil. 130: Michael Latil. 132: Michael Latil. 134-136: Michael Latil.

Props: 10-11: tile, Ikusi Teraky, Sointu, New York; bowl, Sointu; cruets, The American Hand Plus, Washington, D.C.; canister, Uzzolo, Washington, D.C.; silver plate, The American Hand Plus; footed bowl, Platypus, New York; flowerpot, Johnson's Flower Center, Washington, D.C.; skillet, Schiller and Asmus, Inc., Yemassee, S.C.; salt and pepper shakers, Sointu. 13: Christine Steiner. 14: Ron Bower, Jackie Chalkley, Washington, D.C. 15: bowl, Barbara Eigen, New York. 19: Steve Howell, The American Hand Plus. 26: Hutschenreuther Corporation, New York; flatware, Retroneu, New York. 28: Margaret Chatelain, Bristol, Vt. 31: Judith Salomon, The American Hand Plus. 32-33: A Bit of Britain, Alexandria, Va. 36: Gear Stores, New York. 37: Cherishables Antiques, Washington, D.C. 38: Terrafirma Ceramics, Inc., New York. 39: A Bit of Britain. 42: Elayne De Vito. 45: Scott McDowell, Rogers-Tropea, Inc., New York. 48: background flora, Washington Harbor Flowers by Angelo Bonita, Washington, D.C. 49: Skellin and Company, Bethesda, Md.; servers, Retroneu. 51: Charles Nalle, Rogers-Tropea, Inc. 53: Frances Lee Heminway, West Simsbury, Conn. 55: Nambé Mills, Inc., Santa Fe, N. Mex. 57: Martin's of Georgetown, Washington, D.C.; flatware, Retroneu. 59: Ann Gordon; napkin, Nancy Rombro. 61: Gear Stores; servers, Retroneu. 62: Skellin and Company. 64: A Bit of Britain. 67: Barbara WF Miner, Columbus, Ohio. 69: platter, Rob Barnard, Timberville, Va. 70: waffle iron, Lynn A. Asher. 71: Michael Cohen, Jackie Chalkley; fabric, Gossypia, Alexandria, Va. 72: top, Scandinavian Gallery, Washington, D.C. 72: bottom, Williams-Sonoma, Alexandria, Va. 73: Ann Gordon. 74: Ragnar Naess, Brooklyn, N.Y.; background, Michael Latil. 78-79: platter and bowl, Mary George Kronstadt, Washington, D.C.; basket, Johnson's Flower Center; grill, Marty Block; skewers, Ian Eddy, Jackie Chalkley; picnic table, Mary Jane Blandford. 80: Claudia Reese, The Coffee Connection, Washington, D.C. 82: bowls, Nora Pate Studio, San Francisco, Calif. 83: China Closet, Kensington, Md. 84: Steven Hill, Kansas City, Mo. 85: Stephen Kilborn, Jackie Chalkley; bowl, Ron Bower, Jackie Chalkley. 86: Williams-Sonoma, Washington, D.C. 87: Fitz and Floyd, Inc., Dallas, Tex.; flatware, Retroneu. 88: plate, Preferred Stock, Washington, D.C.; bowl, The Flower Designer, Washington, D.C.; placemat and napkin, Abrielle Fine Linens & Lingerie, Washington, D.C. 90: background, Michael Latil. 91: Maggie Creshkoff, Backlog Pottery, Port Deposit, Md. 92: Sandra Selesnick, Full Circle, Alexandria, Va. 95: Cobweb, New York. 96: plates, Gwathmey/Siegel for Swid Powell and Alessi; bowl, The American Hand Plus. 97: platter, Evans & Campbell Antiques, Washington, D.C.; vegetable bowl, Antiques by Ann Brinkley, Washington, D.C.; chutney bowl, Cavalier Antiques, Alexandria, Va.; carving board, Elayne De Vito. 99: Ginza "Things Japanese," Washington, D.C. 101: Joan Tapper. 102: Cobweb. 107: Cobweb. 108: Ruff & Ready Furnishings, Washington, D.C. 110: Peter Kaizer, The American Hand Plus. 114: John Shedd, Uptown Arts, Washington, D.C.; background, Rebecca Johns. 116: Sasaki Crystal, Inc., New York. 123: bowl, Antiques by Ann Brinkley; forks, Skellin and Company; napkins, Abrielle Fine Linens & Lingerie. 130: WILTON Armetale, New York. 133: WILTON Armetale.

Acknowledgments

The index for this book was prepared by Rose Grant. The editors are particularly indebted to the following people for creating recipes for this volume: Melanie Barnard, New Canaan, Ct.; Peter Brett, Washington, D.C.; Nora Carey, Paris; Robert Chambers, New York; Brooke Dojny, Westport, Ct.; Marie Lou, Bethesda, Md.

The editors also wish to thank: Tony Aiello, California Beef Council, Foster City, Ca.; Barbara Anderson, U.S. Department of Agriculture, Alexandria, Va.; Frank H. Baker and H. C. Palmer, Jr., Nutrition Effects Foundation, Shawnee Mission, Ks.; Charles E. Ball, Jr. and Daryl Wilkes, National Cattlemen's Association, Washington, D.C.; Joe Booker, Zamoiski Co., Baltimore, Md.; Jo Calabrese, Royal Worcester Spode Inc., New York; Jackie Chalkley, Washington, D.C.; La Cuisine, Alexandria, Va.; Jeanne Dale, The Pilgrim Glass Corp., New York; Rex Downey, Oxon Hill, Md.; Flowers Unique, Alexandria, Va.; Dennis Garrett and Ed Nash, The American Hand Plus, Washington, D.C.; Giant Foods, Inc., Landover, Md.; Judith Goodkind, Alexandria, Va.; Chong Su Han, Grass Roots Restaurant, Alexandria, Va.; Pollyanna Hayes, American Lamb Council, Denver, Co.; Hilarie Hoting, American Meat Institute, Washington, D.C.; Imperial Produce, Washington, D.C.; Oscar Katov, Food Marketing Institute, Washington, D.C.; Kitchen Bazaar, Washington, D.C.; Kossow Gourmet Produce, Washington, D.C.; Gary Latzman and Kirk Phillips, Retroneu, New York; Leon, Stanley, Evan and Mark Lobel, New York; Magruder's, Inc., Rockville, Md.; Nambé Mills Inc., Santa Fe, N. Mex.; Lisa Ownby, Alexandria, Va.; Prabhu Ponkshe, American Heart Association, Washington, D.C.; C. Kyle and Ruth Randall, Alexandria, Va.; Linda Robertson, JUD Tile, Vienna, Va.; Safeway Stores, Inc., Landover, Md.; WILTON Armetale, New York; Straight from the Crate, Inc., Alexandria, Va.; Sutton Place Gourmet, Washington, D.C.; Ann Vaughan, Jenn-Air Company, Indianapolis, Ind.; Janet Williams, National Livestock and Meat Board, Chicago, Ill.; Williams-Sonoma, Inc., Alexandria, Va., and Washington, D.C.; Lynn Addison Yorke, Cheverly, Md.

The editors wish to thank the following for their donation of kitchen equipment: Le Creuset, distributed by Schiller and Asmus, Inc., Yemasse, S.C.; Cuisinarts, Inc., Greenwich, Conn.; KitchenAid, Inc., Troy, Ohio; Oster, Milwaukee, Wis.